Creamware

THE FABER MONOGRAPHS ON POTTERY AND PORCELAIN

Present Editor: R. J. CHARLESTON
Former Editors: W. B. HONEY, ARTHUR LANE and SIR HARRY GARNER

WORCESTER PORCELAIN AND LUND'S BRISTOL *by* Franklin A. Barrett

DERBY PORCELAIN *by* Franklin A. Barrett
and Arthur L. Thorpe

APOTHECARY JARS *by* R. E. A. Drey

ENGLISH DELFTWARE *by* F. H. Garner *and* Michael Archer

ORIENTAL BLUE AND WHITE *by* Sir Harry Garner

KOREAN POTTERY AND PORCELAIN OF THE YI PERIOD
by G. St. G. M. Gompertz

MASON PORCELAIN AND IRONSTONE
by Reginald Haggar *and* Elizabeth Adams

NEW HALL AND ITS IMITATORS *by* David Holgate

FRENCH PORCELAIN OF THE EIGHTEENTH CENTURY
by W. B. Honey

LATER CHINESE PORCELAIN *by* Soame Jenyns

JAPANESE POTTERY *by* Soame Jenyns

ENGLISH PORCELAIN FIGURES OF THE EIGHTEENTH CENTURY
by Arthur Lane

FRENCH FAIENCE *by* Arthur Lane

GREEK POTTERY *by* Arthur Lane

LATER ISLAMIC POTTERY *by* Arthur Lane

YÜAN PORCELAIN AND STONEWARE *by* Margaret Medley

MEDIEVAL ENGLISH POTTERY *by* Bernard Rackham

ARTIST POTTERS IN ENGLAND *by* Muriel Rose

ENGLISH BLUE AND WHITE PORCELAIN OF THE EIGHTEENTH CENTURY
by Bernard Watney

LONGTON HALL PORCELAIN *by* Bernard Watney

CREAMWARE

BY

DONALD TOWNER

FABER AND FABER

London & Boston

First published in 1978
by Faber and Faber Limited
3 Queen Square London WC1
Printed in Great Britain by
BAS Printers Limited, Over Wallop, Hampshire
All rights reserved

© Donald Towner, 1978

British Library Cataloguing in Publication Data

Towner, Donald
   Creamware. – (The Faber monographs on
   pottery and porcelain.)
   1. Pottery, English – History
   I. Title
   738.3'7   NK4085
ISBN 0-571-04964-8

CONTENTS

CONTENTS

COLOUR PLATES AND
LINE-DRAWINGS

FOREWORD

In eighteenth-century England two main types of pottery competed for supremacy. One, tin-glazed earthenware (commonly called 'delftware' in England) depended for its appeal on its white glaze and painted decoration, but suffered from the practical inconvenience that its soft body chipped readily in use. The second, deriving ultimately from the indigenous English potting tradition of previous centuries, and centred chiefly in Staffordshire, was divided into two main technical families.

The first of these, salt-glazed stoneware, grafted on to the main stock towards the end of the seventeenth century, culminated in the third quarter of the eighteenth century in a white ware decorated by moulding, painting or printing. Recommended by its durability and its oblique reference to the whiteness of porcelain, it enjoyed great popularity in England and her colonies, and on the Continent of Europe. The second branch, lead-glazed earthenware, firing at a considerably lower temperature, was descended without break from the medieval tradition, but was obliged in the course of the first half of the eighteenth century to improve and refine itself in order to survive in a highly competitive market. White clays strengthened by the addition of calcined flints, and refined glazes, produced a pottery which rivalled stoneware in the very qualities on which it had depended for its predominance. The lightness and smoothness of this 'cream-coloured earthenware' gave it practical advantages which brought it to the fore at a psychologically critical moment, when the rococo style in the decorative arts was yielding ground to the neoclassical mode popularized above all by the Adam brothers in architecture and interior decoration. Wedgwood was the ceramic protagonist in this movement, and one branch of his business (and the more important commercially) lay in the field of the cream-coloured earthenware which he had helped to perfect. To it, as to his unglazed coloured stonewares, he applied decoration in the rising taste, and the two helped each other to an unprecedented popularity. Creamware, it was recorded, was to be found in every inn from Russia to Spain. It was England's greatest contribution to the art and technology of pottery, and gave the death-blow to tin-glazed earthenware both in England and on the Continent.

Mr. Towner has been the leading pioneer in the research which has in the past twenty years revolutionized our knowledge of this branch of pottery. Whereas then everything which was not otherwise marked was attributed either to Leeds or to Wedgwood, today it is possible to discriminate between a number of provincial centres which made the ware with slight differences of quality, colour, shape and decoration. The present book charts these developments, as well as tracing the impact of creamware on the Continent of Europe.

R. J. CHARLESTON

ACKNOWLEDGEMENTS

In addition to the acknowledgements expressed at the beginning of *English Cream-coloured Earthenware*, it gives me very real pleasure to acknowledge the parts played by so many of my friends in the production of this book.

First, I would like to thank Mr. Robert Charleston as editor of the Faber monographs on ceramics, as former Keeper of Ceramics at the Victoria and Albert Museum, and above all as a friend, for all the help and encouragement he has given me, not only with this book, but at all times. I would also like to express my great appreciation of the unfailing help given me by all the staff of the Ceramics Department of the Victoria and Albert Museum. The friendliness and help given me by the staffs of museums generally has made research such a pleasurable undertaking. Among those whose co-operation I would particularly like to acknowledge with gratitude are Mr. Hugh Tait of the British Museum, Mr. Michael Parkinson of the City of Manchester Art Galleries, Mr. Peter Walton of the Leeds Art Galleries, Miss Sheenah Smith of the Castle Museum Norwich, Mr. Arnold Mountford of the Hanley Museum, Mr. John Austen of Colonial Williamsburg and the Syndics of the Fitzwilliam Museum, Cambridge.

After the sale of such a large part of my collection at Sotheby's in February 1968, it has been difficult to ascertain who the present owners are. Where such pieces have been illustrated in the present book the owners' names have been given wherever possible, otherwise I have only been able to say that they were formerly in my collection, much as I should have liked to have acknowledged their present ownership.

I would also like to thank Mr. David Zeitlin for allowing me to illustrate some of the many pieces he acquired from my collection at the sale, also Mr. Tom Walford for allowing me to illustrate his lovely Melbourne tureen in colour and other pieces in black and white from his fine creamware collection.

Others to whom I must express my gratitude for allowing me to illustrate their pieces are: Mr. Byron Born; the legatees of the late Sir Victor and Lady Gollancz and the trustees of the late T. Murray Ragg.

Above all I would like to express my deep sense of gratitude to Faber & Faber for undertaking to publish this book thereby bringing it to fruition.

PREFACE

English Cream-coloured Earthenware by the present author was published in 1957 by Faber and Faber in their series of monographs on ceramics. Since then a great many new facts about this class of ware and the potters who made it, have been discovered. Excavations have brought to light the wares of potteries previously unknown to us and in some instances a fresh assessment has had to be made, while further knowledge of those already treated has been acquired. It was felt, therefore, that rather than publish a revised edition of *English Cream-coloured Earthenware*, a new book was needed which included the most up-to-date information, with fresh chapters, drawings and plates, but retaining wherever possible those passages in the original book which might be considered still to retain their value. Accordingly the present book has been given the title *Creamware* as the name more generally used for this class of ware today and which may be considered more suitable particularly in view of a chapter it contains which deals entirely with Continental creamware.

Donald Towner

Chapter 1

INTRODUCTION

Creamware, known in the eighteenth century as cream-coloured earthenware or cream-colour, was the direct descendant of the lead-glazed wares of the Middle Ages. English pottery, through the ages, had become successively more refined, more technically perfect and more artistically excellent until it reached its climax in the creamware of the eighteenth century with its fine form, thin body, clean and brilliant glaze which formed a perfect background for the ingenious, harmonious and free painting of the earthenware enamellers of that time. It was the prototype of the white-glazed earthenware that is manufactured today. At its best it did not seek to imitate porcelain either in colour, form or decoration, but remained essentially true to its English earthenware tradition. Even when the creamware potters sought inspiration from the work of the silversmith, the metal forms were freely adapted to form a more plastic idiom suitable to the clay medium. So traditional was the creamware that it would be truer to say that it evolved from the main stream of English pottery than that it was invented at any particular time.

Earthenware that was cream in colour was made from the beginning of the eighteenth century. At first the potters coated a darker body with a cream-coloured slip, but by the importation of clays from Dorset and Devonshire, together with the introduction of calcined flint, the manufacture of creamware was made possible.[1] These materials when fired to a temperature high enough to form a stoneware produced the white salt-glazed ware or 'white stoneware' as it used to be called. Salt, which was thrown into the kiln during the process of firing, volatilized and formed a vitreous silicate on the surface of the ware. The same materials, however, when fired to a lower temperature and glazed with lead, formed the cream-coloured earthenware. This was first produced some time before 1740. At this time the lead powder or galena, mixed with a certain amount of ground flint, was dusted on the ware, which was then given its one and only firing. This process produced an extremely brilliant

---

[1] It has been stated that John Astbury first introduced calcined flint into the body of the ware in 1720. Its use, however, is recorded by John Dwight in one of his notebooks (British Museum) as early as 1698.

transparent glaze of a rich cream colour. Small stamped motifs similar to those found on saltglaze and redware were sometimes applied to the cream-colour of this time.[1] Dry crystals of metallic oxides such as copper, iron and manganese, were frequently dusted on, probably with the tip of a brush. These dissolved during the firing and mixing with the lead ran in a charming, but somewhat uncontrolled manner, to form touches of coloured decoration (Plates 3A and 4). This form of decoration led directly to the 'tortoiseshell' and other wares with coloured glazes. The method employed at this time of producing the cream-coloured ware was found to be unsatisfactory as the lead powder produced poisoning among the potters, and the grinding of the flint stones a disease known as potter's rot. Patents were therefore taken out by Thomas Benson between 1726 and 1732 for grinding the flint stones in water, and about 1740 a fluid glaze was invented, probably by Enoch Booth of Tunstall, Staffordshire, in which the lead and flint were both mixed and ground in water. The method was adopted of first firing the ware to a biscuit, and then glazing and re-firing it. The date usually given for this invention is 1750, but in actual fact it must have taken place about ten years earlier (see page 23). Having described the chief developments which resulted in the double-fired creamware coated with a fluid glaze, I must point out that this did not immediately displace the previous types. Thus creamware with small applied reliefs touched in with underglaze colours was made at least as late as 1761, the year of the marriage of King George III, which event was sometimes depicted on this type of ware. Tortoiseshell and other wares with coloured glazes as well as salt-glazed stoneware continued to be made in quantity till late in the century.

Great developments were made in the creamware about the middle of the century and by 1760 the ware was already being enamelled and had a rapidly increasing market which during the next few years was to spread to the Continent as well. At this time much of the creamware was being made by the saltglaze potters, and painted by the saltglaze enamellers. It therefore bore a strong resemblance to the saltglaze ware both in form and decoration. Teapots were globular in shape with crabstock handles and spouts (Plate 7A); coffee-pots were pear-shaped with magnificent rococo handles and spouts (Plates 4 and 5). The colour was a deep cream almost amounting to buff and was derived not only from the body but also from the glaze, the latter usually being either a deep yellow, a soft brown or a bright lemon-yellow with a tinge of green, though one of the earliest glazes on creamware was of a bluish tint. As would be expected, it was during this early period of the ware that the greatest vigour, freedom and originality were shown, while the full possibilities of the material were as yet undiscovered. Foremost of the pioneers in Staffordshire who availed themselves of Enoch Booth's invention was Thomas Whieldon.

[1] Some small creamware teapots decorated with coffee-coloured applied stamped ornaments similar in pattern to those found on some early salt-glazed stoneware, may perhaps be attributable to this period. Examples of this type of creamware are at the Castle Museum, Norwich.

Creamware was not, however, confined to Staffordshire; in fact it has become evident that saltglaze potters were working in a number of large potting centres outside Staffordshire such as Derbyshire, Liverpool, Yorkshire and Swansea, and wherever this was so, the manufacture of creamware was developed to the eventual exclusion of the salt-glazed stoneware.

By 1751 an improved creamware is stated to have been made by the Warburtons. Ten years later Josiah Wedgwood was directing all his efforts towards its development and by 1763 he was producing a considerably refined ware of a much paler colour. By 1768 he had transformed the creamware into virtually a new substance of great beauty, which combined lightness with strength and was capable of the greatest delicacy of workmanship. There were, no doubt, many contributing factors towards this great change in creamware, but first and foremost was the introduction of china-clay and china-stone from Cornwall into the body and glaze. The glaze used by Wedgwood at this time was a yellowish-green colour which may be seen in crevices where it lies more thickly. By 1770 other Staffordshire potters were producing the light-coloured creamware to which Wedgwood had given the name 'Queen's ware'. Elsewhere potters continued to make the deeper-coloured creamware for some years afterwards, usually till about 1775. A letter from Wedgwood on page 44 shows that the creamware potteries, at this time at any rate, made either the deep or pale creamware, but were unable for practical reasons to make both simultaneously.

Only a few minor changes in the development of creamware were made after this. Of importance, however, was a considerable increase about 1780 in the production of creamware, the glaze of which was tinged with blue. This glaze when applied to a somewhat modified creamware body produced a ware that was slightly greyish in appearance and is usually referred to as pearlware. In this type of ware the bluish glaze was somewhat at variance with the warm-coloured body and although much of it was extremely pleasing, on the whole it was less satisfactory aesthetically than the true creamware with its greenish or yellowish glazes.

The attribution of pieces of creamware to a particular factory has always been a difficulty, as virtually no creamware was marked prior to Josiah Wedgwood's manufacture of it in Burslem. In 1772, however, Wedgwood wrote to Thomas Bentley proposing that all his ware should be marked, but even after that date a considerable quantity of his ware seems to have missed being stamped. Other factories were for the most part content to leave their wares unmarked, largely due, no doubt, to the practice of supplying each other with wares to supplement exhausted stocks. The difficulty of attribution is further increased by the similarity of both body and glaze of the creamware made by a number of potteries as well as by the interchange and copying of ideas. Nor can we be helped to any great extent by the enamelled decoration, as with but a few exceptions factories sent their creamware to outside enamellers for decoration so that one enameller might decorate the ware of a number of potters. The practice of enamelling creamware at the factory itself was only gradually adopted. It follows therefore, that there is a great deal in the present subject that awaits confirmation and further discovery. It must be pointed out, however, that little progress can be made unless the whole field of creamware manufacture is kept in view.

Chapter 2
EARLY STAFFORDSHIRE POTTERS

ENOCH BOOTH

Master Potter at Tunstall, Staffordshire

Enoch Booth was a saltglaze potter who decorated his ware with that form of decoration known as 'scratch-blue'. Fortunately he signed and dated some of his ware; and it should be noted that he was one of the very few saltglaze potters who ever did so. This may be an indication of the experimental nature of his work. A scratch-blue saltglaze mug in the Glaisher Collection at Cambridge is inscribed 'Enoch Booth 1742' (see mark 1, page 218). A loving-cup also in scratch-blue saltglaze at the Hanley Museum is inscribed 'E.B. 1750' (see mark 2, page 218). A creamware punch-bowl in the British Museum is inscribed 'E.B. 1743' (see mark 3, page 218) (Plates 1A and B). There is very little doubt that this punch-bowl was also made by Enoch Booth, and from what has already been said it is apparent that he continued his manufacture of saltglaze while experimenting with the new creamware. This magnificent bowl which is ten inches in diameter is painted in underglaze blue in reserved panels against a ground finely speckled with manganese purple. A teapot of a similar body and glaze and with the identical style of underglaze painting is in the possession of Mr. W. Grant-Davidson (Plate 2A), while another is in the Hanley Museum. Neither of these are signed or dated but they are both clearly by the same hand as the British Museum bowl.

THOMAS WHIELDON

Born at Stoke 1719; Master Potter at Fenton Low 1740; Little Fenton (Fenton Vivian) and Fenton Hall, Staffordshire 1749; died 1795

Thomas Whieldon has always been regarded as one of the greatest English potters. Young and aspiring potters of the day sought to associate themselves

IA PUNCH-BOWL. Reserved panels painted in underglaze blue on a finely speckled manganese ground
ENOCH BOOTH, 1743, diam. 10 in (25.5 cm)
British Museum. See page 23
IB Underside of IA

2A TEAPOT. Reserved panels painted in manganese brown and underglaze blue on a
finely speckled manganese ground
ENOCH BOOTH, about 1743, ht. 3½ in (18 cm)
Grant-Davidson Collection. See page 23

2B TEAPOT, painted in underglaze colours. Spout, handle and feet solid agate
WHIELDON, about 1745, ht. 4¾ in (12 cm)
Formerly Gollancz Collection. See page 28

with him to learn his methods. So we find Greatbatch,[1] Garner and Spode among his apprentices, while the young Josiah Wedgwood in 1754 at the age of twenty-four entered into a partnership with him chiefly to study glazes. In 1740 Whieldon acquired a pot-works at Fenton Low which from 1750 he let to William Meir, Edward Warburton and others, he having established his pottery by that time at Little Fenton (sometimes known as Fenton Vivian),[2] on the south side of the main road to Uttoxeter, though he himself lived at Penkhull, rather more than a mile to the west. In 1749 Whieldon acquired Fenton Hall as well. He had evidently become a rich man and is believed to have retired by about 1780. In 1786 he was appointed High Sheriff of Staffordshire and died in 1795.

In the past a great many different kinds of ware have been attributed to Whieldon. Excavations took place at Fenton Low in 1925 where, as was only to be expected, a great many different types of ware were found. Most of these were wasters from the potters to whom Whieldon had let the Fenton Low pot-works. There were however pieces which by their style could be ascribed to the few years following 1740 when Whieldon himself was working there, and amongst these were some pieces of creamware having a rich golden glaze.

In 1969 the discovery of a document lead to the excavation of Whieldon's main pottery site at Fenton Vivian. The shards found there can be divided into two sections—those from the upper and those from the lower layers. The division between these two groups can be approximately estimated as those made before and those made after the year 1760. The shards found in the lower layers confirmed previous opinion as to the types of ware Whieldon produced before 1760. Apart from redware and saltglaze shards, these consisted very largely of a colour-glazed ware, which, known as 'tortoiseshell' ware, has long been associated with the name of Whieldon and is a creamware decorated with coloured glazes giving a mottled effect (Plate 3A). As we know from excavated material, these glazes were not painted on but applied to the body in crystal form. During the firing the crystals melted and merged into the glaze, producing the mottling. The following bill to Thomas Fletcher from Whieldon's notebook at the City Museum, Stoke-on-Trent, clearly indicates, however, that Whieldon was making creamware as distinct from his tortoiseshell ware and that some of this bore painted decoration.

Mr. Thomas Fletcher Dr.

Nov. 7. 1749

To			
	1 Doz plates Tor	8	0
	2-¼ Do plane	2	6
	2 2 dish	2	–
	1 do painted	2	–
	1 do Creamcol:	1	8
	5 pails	2	6

[1] William Greatbatch became Whieldon's chief modeller, in succession to Aaron Wood.
[2] For an account of the discovery of Whieldon's works at Fenton Vivian, see 'Thomas Whieldon's Manufactory at Fenton Vivian', by Arnold Mountford, *E.C.C. Transactions*, Vol. 8, Part 2, 1972.

3A MUG. Tortoiseshell ware, mottled with brown manganese
WHIELDON, about 1750, ht. 3 in (7.6 cm) *Towner Collection*
TEAPOT. Applied vine pattern in relief, mottled with brown manganese
WHIELDON, about 1750, ht. 3 in (7.6 cm)
Zeitlin Collection. See pages 26 and 28

3B SUGAR-BOWL. Uncoloured creamware with applied gilded reliefs
WHIELDON, about 1750, ht. 3¼ in (8.25 cm)
Formerly Towner Collection. See page 28

'Tor' in the first item was an abbreviation frequently used by Whieldon for 'Tortoiseshell'. The meaning of it therefore is, one dozen tortoiseshell plates, eight shillings. By $2\frac{1}{4}$ dozen plain plates in the next item, it is probable that undecorated creamware plates are meant. Below this is an item the meaning of which may be obscure to many, but it means two teapots of the two–dish size, that is to say, that will hold two dishes or cups of tea.[1] This item, it will be seen, affects the two following ones which could be read: 'one painted teapot to hold two cups and one creamware teapot of the same size.' The last item refers to ice-pails. The kind of painting of the teapot just referred to would almost certainly have been painting in underglaze colours such as we find on some rare pieces of creamware of about the date of this bill. This consists of landscape, flower or figure painting in brown sometimes with green or blue (Plate 2B).

Much of the early Whieldon creamware whether plain or tortoiseshell, bore sprigged decoration, that is to say small patterns, usually floral, in relief, applied from moulds after the pot had been thrown. These were frequently joined by clay threads forming stems, or so arranged as to form a single unit (Plates 3A and B, and Colour Plate A) or were touched in with colour or gold (Plates 3B and 4). Teapots at this time frequently had a bird knob and stood on three feet, the handle and spout being crabstock. Sometimes we meet with early examples of Whieldon creamware on which the absolute plainness is relieved by a very gentle use of coloured glazes. The refinement of such pieces is very pleasing. Much of the recently excavated material from the lower layers of the Fenton Vivian site, apart from saltglaze, blackware and redware, of which there was an abundance, consisted of colour-glazed creamware in which brown, green, blue-grey, charcoal-grey and yellow were used. This probably dates from the early 1750s, and it may have been these coloured glazes that led Josiah Wedgwood to seek a connexion with Whieldon in order to study and experiment with them (Plate 5).

The partnership between Whieldon and Wedgwood was formed in 1754 under curious terms such as the provision that Wedgwood would be under no obligation to reveal to anyone the results of his experiments. These, as he himself states, were carried out at Fenton Hall, but the pottery at Fenton Vivian seems to have remained the works for general production purposes.

During the five years of the partnership much of the ware produced was made in imitation of fruit and vegetables such as cauliflowers, apples, pears, melons and pineapples (Plates 7A and B). In this the partners were adopting the fashion of the day which started on the Continent whence it influenced English porcelain factories such as Chelsea and Longton Hall. In the Whieldon-Wedgwood and the later Wedgwood versions of this type of ware in particular, the body often ceased to be creamware in the true sense of the word and was in fact what Wedgwood himself describes as 'common earthenware'. If pieces of this type of ware are examined they will be seen to be coarser, rougher and

---

[1] See letter from W. Greatbatch, page 36, 'Please send by bearer a 2 dish Tpt. with the queen printed upon.'

4   COFFEE-POT. Applied reliefs touched with coloured glazes
Probably WHIELDON, about 1755, ht. $7\frac{1}{2}$ in (19 cm)
Victoria and Albert Museum. See page 28

greyer in the actual body. Early pieces, however, which are almost certainly by
Whieldon before the partnership period are still creamware.

Whieldon's wares influenced potters throughout the country, and colour-
glazed and tortoiseshell wares were produced at Liverpool, Leeds, Derby and
elsewhere. To distinguish between some of these and Whieldon's own
productions is sometimes difficult, but as a rule the surest means lies in the
form and details of the ware itself, though a number of potteries had their own
distinctive technique in applying the colour-glazes.

Among the shards found on the Whieldon site at Fenton Vivian were some
of a much paler creamware, and it may be that these were made either a little

before or soon after the termination of the partnership period. One of these is a cover for a teapot of the well-known pattern in which the teapot is modelled as a basket of fruit and touched in with a number of underglaze colours. Besides being a pale creamware pieces of this pattern are moulded, not thrown, with applied reliefs added in the manner of Whieldon's earlier wares. It should be noted, however, that this pattern was copied by a number of other factories. Another type of pale creamware of which shards were found on the Whieldon site had vertical stripes in underglaze green. Quite an amount of this kind of ware was found, some of which had borders of pearl-beading, which again suggests its not having been made till about 1760 or even later. This type was also made by a number of potteries including Leeds (Plate 83B), Castleford, Neale and Co., Melbourne and Cockpit Hill. In all these further cases this ware was not made much before 1780. The green on the Whieldon pieces is slightly more yellow than the green of other factories.

In addition to the types of ware already described a number of figures are attributed to Whieldon. The figure of a Turk illustrated (Plate 6) is in creamware coated with rich colour glazes. This particular model also occurs in both plain and coloured saltglaze and was copied from a Meissen model by J. J. Kaendler. It may be that this figure is the work of Aaron Wood, Whieldon's principal modeller.

Line drawings of some of the knobs and other moulded details from the lower layers of the Fenton Vivian site are shown in Appendix I (Plate VIII). All these were discovered in quantity.

It has long been a matter of speculation as to what Whieldon produced after Wedgwood left him in 1759. Jewitt in his *Ceramic Art* states: 'In 1759 the partnership expired; Wedgwood returned to Burslem, and Whieldon continued the business alone.' There is no possible reason to think otherwise; but how much longer he continued to work at Fenton Vivian is not known. After a thorough investigation of the shards at the Hanley Museum excavated from the upper soil of the Whieldon site at Fenton Vivian, and after discussions with those responsible for the excavations, it became abundantly clear that most of the shards found there were not wasters from the pottery, but consisted of wares from a number of potters working elsewhere and included household breakages, all of which had been pitched in and dug over many times with subsequent building and drainage. It follows therefore that no reliance can be placed on these shards that they are of Whieldon's manufacture.

A further pottery site was excavated recently at Fenton. The creamware shards from this pottery, both glazed and unglazed, suggest that it was being worked about the middle of the eighteenth century, by a potter whose name, at present, we do not know. A first examination of the shards would seem to indicate that this pottery was the source of at least some of the small teapots, cups and jugs of plain creamware decorated with stamped reliefs applied to the piece and touched in with dark brown slip. Two teapots in this group, the origin of which has long been a problem, are at the Castle Museum, Norwich.

5 COFFEE-POT, clouded with soft brown manganese
Probably WHIELDON, about 1750, ht. 6⅝ in (16.9)
Victoria and Albert Museum. See page 28

THE WARBURTONS OF HOT LANE, COBRIDGE

*John Warburton 1720–61; Anne Warburton (née Daniel) 1713–98, Master
Potter 1761*

Soon after 1740, Cobridge became the centre of the enamelling industry which
sprang into existence when it was discovered that the fine white saltglaze
formed a suitable surface for enamel painting. At first enamelling on saltglaze
and creamware was a specialized industry, and in some cases the potter might

have to send his ware a considerable distance to be enamelled. The Warburtons of Hot Lane, Cobridge, were an exception to this, for they are reputed to have been not only pioneers of creamware manufacture but also enamellers of considerable ability.

John Warburton married Anne Daniel. The Daniels were a neighbouring family of enamellers, also of Hot Lane, Cobridge.[1] After John's death in 1761, Anne became master potter.

In his *History of the Staffordshire Potteries* published in 1829, Simeon Shaw states, 'In 1751 were the last improvements of Cream Colour (prior to those of the late Mr. Wedgwood) by Mrs. Warburton of Hot Lane.' Also, 'Mr Wedgwood employed a waggon once a fortnight to take down a load of cream colour to be printed by Messrs. Sadler and Green of Liverpool . . . the teaware required to be painted was sent to Mrs. Warburton in Hot Lane and some time elapsed before Mr. Wedgwood had the enamelling done on his own premises.' In spite of this indication, not one example of Anne Warburton's creamware or enamelling can now be identified with certainty. A considerable correspondence between Wedgwood and the Warburtons is amongst the records kept at Keele University Library. This shows that buying and selling took place between them and there are numerous bills, but no mention is made of any enamelling, and in view of the fact that we know Wedgwood was sending his creamware to Leeds to be enamelled by 1763, Shaw's statement that Wedgwood's tea-ware was enamelled by Mrs. Warburton cannot be taken as a correct statement, though it is possible that she may have been responsible for a small amount such as the teapot on Plate 12A.

Many descendants of John and Anne Warburton became potters of repute. Among these, their son Jacob (1741–1826) became one of the original partners of the New Hall works, while Peter and Francis Warburton, grandsons of John and Anne, manufactured some very fine creamware at their Cobridge works. This was a rich cream in colour with a yellowish glaze. Some pieces are marked 'P and F. Warburton', either in capitals or lower-case lettering (Appendix III, marks 129, 130, 131). Some remarkably fine cruets with well-modelled figures forming the centre, can be ascribed to them (Plate 37). Francis Warburton set up a factory—La Charité-sur-Loire, Nièvre, France—in 1802 (see page 184).

POMONA WORKS, NEWCASTLE-UNDER-LYME

Excavations which have recently taken place on the site of the Pomona works at Newcastle-under-Lyme, which were founded by Samuel Bell in 1724–5, show that a fine creamware was being produced there about the middle of the eighteenth century. A creamware cup in Dr. Watney's collection exactly

[1] Very little is known of the productions of the Daniels. A cake-basket of fine quality creamware and signed 'John Daniel, 1775' is at the British Museum (Appendix III, mark 101). John Daniel (1756–1821) was the son of Ralph Daniel of Cobridge, and nephew to Anne Warburton.

6 FIGURE OF A TURK, after the Meissen porcelain figure by Kaendler. Clouded with brown and green colour glazes
WHIELDON, about 1755, ht. 7½ in (19 cm)
Victoria and Albert Museum. See page 30

matches a shard found on the Pomona works site. It is deep cream in colour with a crabstock handle and has slightly curvilinear fluting over which raised prunus blossom has been sprigged on and touched with gold (see illustration in *E.C.C. Transactions*, Vol. 9, Part 1, 1973, Plate 9B).

WILLIAM GREATBATCH
AND THE EARLY WEDGWOOD WARES

From 1749 William Greatbatch was apprentice and afterwards modeller to Thomas Whieldon at Fenton Vivian, Staffordshire. When the Whieldon-Wedgwood partnership was dissolved in 1759, Greatbatch left Whieldon and began work at Lower Lane, Fenton, under an agreement to supply wares to Josiah Wedgwood. It becomes evident from the correspondence between the two men that Wedgwood realized the inventive genius of Greatbatch and looked to him for wares of novel and ingenious designs until such time as his own position was secured. The wares made by Greatbatch, which were of a common earthenware body as well as some of a fine creamware, were delivered to Wedgwood in the biscuit state ready to be glazed. Greatbatch moved to Lane Delph in 1764, and the following letter seems to mean that he supplied ware to Wedgwood similar to that made by Whieldon.

> Lane Delph, May 1764. To Mr. Josiah Wedgwood.
> There are ready two of the crates of Pine Apple ware and a large quantity of plates about a gross & 1–2 of light colour teapots and a good quantity of China tpts. the same as Mr. Whieldon & other sorts.

By 'China tpts.' he undoubtedly refers to teapots, usually hexagonal, with Chinese motifs in relief (Plate 9A). Greatbatch seems to use the words 'China' and 'Chinese' indiscriminately. Teapots of this kind were usually of a somewhat coarse earthenware decorated with clouded underglaze colours; some rare examples exist, however, which are of a fine quality creamware painted in enamel colours (Plate 9B). It is tempting to think that the two following letters have a direct reference to teapots of this type.

> Lower Lane, Dec. 9th. 1763
> I have sent you a square China Teapot as a specimen, should be glad to have your judgment on it the couler is light I own but dare ingage to make any quantity of a darker Couler if required.
> Wm. Greatbatch.

> Dec. 12th. 1763.
> I have received yours wrote by Mr. Byerley and have made a new handle and spout to the China Teapot. Wm. Greatbatch.

The following bill will give an idea of the variety of wares Greatbatch supplied to Wedgwood.

July 22nd. 1760.

    3 Foxglove teapts.[1]   12s.

    2 Large Leaves

    7 Pr. Cornu Copias

    3 Pr. Large fluted Candlesticks

    2 Melon sauce Bts & stds.

    2 Leaf candlesticks

    2 fluted tpts.

    2 Mossaic Do.

    2 Woodbine do.

    4 Green do.

    2 Chinese do.

    5 Doz Large Toys

Left at the Cross Keys Wood Street
London.

In addition to these patterns, some of which are quite unknown to us today, it is apparent from the correspondence that Greatbatch also supplied Wedgwood with ware in the form of cauliflowers, pineapples, apples, pears, quinces, melons and other fruits (Plate 7B). Green teapots mentioned in the bill may refer to teapots to be coloured green rather than those already glazed and were, no doubt, the well-known teapots entirely covered on the outside with a fine deep green glaze, the inside sometimes disclosing a fine quality creamware (Plate 8A).[2] Gilding was frequently added. There is a tradition that Greatbatch modelled the saltglaze wall-vases in the form of a cornucopia with a bust of 'Flora' in relief,[3] and this seems to be well borne out by facts. Four-sided tea-caddies made from the same mould as the 'Flora' wall-vase are of probable Greatbatch origin. These have the same rich cream glaze as the hexagonal teapots already referred to, which is quite distinct from the greenish glazes of Wedgwood.

A pattern for which Greatbatch was partly responsible was the 'shell', which was used so much by Wedgwood and copied by others. A creamware shell-pattern spout was excavated at Fenton Low and is now in the Castle Museum, Norwich. The same spout also occurs on an enamelled teapot formerly in the author's collection and now in the Leeds Art Galleries (Plate 16B) and on a beautiful, deep green teapot in the Glaisher Collection, Cambridge, as well as on teapots of other makes (see Appendix I, Plate II:3). The following letter, however, probably refers to a more elaborate type of shell pattern which occurs on some of Wedgwood's creamware (see Appendix I, Plate II:2):

[1] Saltglaze moulds for 'foxglove' and 'Chinese' pattern teapots are in the Wedgwood Museum, Barlaston, and saltglaze dishes of the 'foxglove' pattern both plain and coloured are in the Schreiber Collection, Victoria and Albert Museum.

[2] In 1763 Wedgwood was obtaining copper scales to form this green glaze from Robinson & Rhodes of Leeds (see page 50).

[3] A mould for these is at the Wedgwood Museum, Barlaston.

Sir,

  Desire you'll send six guineas by the Bearer hereof and you'll greatly oblige your humble servant.

Wm. Greatbatch.

P.S. I expected your advice in the shape of the Teapots agreed on. The work is complicated for the shell and other teapot. Should be glad you would cut the shape upon paper you would have them to be and whether you would have a ground upon them or not.

Saturday noon Lower Lane.

To Mr. Josiah Wedgwood, Burslem.

The correspondence also shows that Greatbatch bought small quantities of transfer-printed ware from Wedgwood for which he paid in cash.

Lane Delf Sept. 16. 1763.

Please to send by bearer a 2 dish Tpt. with the queen printed upon.

The following letter is also of interest as evidence that Greatbatch modelled teapots in the shape of fruits for Wedgwood. These were afterwards decorated by Wedgwood in underglaze colours:

Lower Lane Friday noon.

Sir,

  Please to send word by the Bearer whether we shou'd or not have sent you an apple Tpt. shou'd be glad to know if you wou'd have leaves on the side the same as use to be, send a Tpt with Earl Bute on it, have sent Cash to pay for it.

The following letter to Wedgwood shows that ware to be enamelled was sent to a Mr. Courzen for that purpose:

Lower Lane. 12 July 1763

Sir,

  I shall send Mr. Courzen's ware to his painting shop to Night.

Wm. Greatbatch.

Greatbatch continued to work for Wedgwood at Lane Delph for some time. According to a letter written by Thomas Byerley to Josiah Wedgwood the second, Greatbatch later worked for John Turner of Lane End, but the dates of his employment there are not known.

The following entries are from the *London Gazette*:

Feb. 1782
    Bankrupt—William Greatbatch, potter,
            Stoke-on-Trent.

26 April 1788
    Bankrupt—William Greatbatch, potter,
            Stoke.

7A   TEAPOT, in the form of an apple, coloured with manganese brown
WHIELDON, about 1755, ht. 3⅞ in (10 cm)
Victoria and Albert Museum. See page 28

7B   TEAPOT, in the form of a melon, decorated with green and yellow glazes
WEDGWOOD, about 1763, ht. 4 in (10.2 cm)
Victoria and Albert Museum. See pages 28, 35 and 43

In 1788 he went to ask for assistance at Etruria, as a result of which it would seem he was employed there in receipting the deliveries of clay to the factory.

Dr. Simeon Shaw on page 190 of his *History of the Staffordshire Potteries* published in 1829 writes:

> Another excellent modeller, in fact a general workman of first rate abilities, was Mr. William Greatbatch sometime employed by Messrs. Whieldon and Wedgwood and had commenced business on his own account at the manufactory at Fenton, now a small part of Bourne, Baker & Bourne where he produced numerous articles of improved patterns and kinds and for some time had a rapid sale of teapots on which was printed in black by Thomas Radford the history of the 'Prodigal Son' but heavy losses at length ruined him. Mr. Wedgwood aware of the talents of his former servant engaged him for life at the very high wages of five shillings a day whether at work or play, and a house rent free which sum was regularly paid him till his death, though he survived his master.

The teapots mentioned in this statement of Simeon Shaw's form part of a very large group of creamware, examples from which are illustrated (Plates 35 and 36). Some of the teapots in this group have the following inscription printed upon them, 'Published as the Act directs Jany 4 1778 by W. Greatbatch Lane-Delf Staffordshire' (Plate 36B) (Appendix III: mark 39), while on others in the same group, the name 'Greatbatch' only, appears as part of the engraving. The inscription 'Published as the Act directs' followed by the date and a name, was frequently inscribed at the foot of engravings. The name refers to that of the publisher, but sometimes the engraver and the publisher were one and the same person. A single name by itself in an engraving usually denotes the engraver, though the printer's name or the name of the factory sometimes occurs, but in such cases, these are usually placed a little apart from the engraving itself. Thomas Radford, referred to in Simeon Shaw's statement, worked as an engraver at Cockpit Hill, Derby, probably till it closed down in 1779. If one compares Radford's signed engravings on Derby creamware with those of the 'Prodigal Son' series, which are clearly all by one hand, a considerable difference of style and technique will be apparent. It would seem therefore, that little credence should be given to Simeon Shaw's statement that the 'Prodigal Son' series was 'printed in black by Thomas Radford'. Our only alternative therefore is to accept the evidence of the signature that the engraver was William Greatbatch.[1] If we examine the teapots themselves, it will be noticed that they are not all of one manufacture. This precludes William Greatbatch from having made them all. A transfer-printed teapot of this group at the Victoria and Albert Museum, is of Wedgwood manufacture (Plate 23B)

---

[1] Parish registers at Stoke Parish Church show the following families bringing children to be baptized during the 1730s. Daniel Greatbatch had three children: Joseph, Isaac and Daniel and perhaps others. Isaac and Elizabeth were living at Bury Hill. This Isaac was probably the farmer of 'Berryhill' referred to by Simeon Shaw as the father of William Greatbatch. It should be

8A TEAPOT, coated with a green glaze and decorated with gilded applied reliefs
    WEDGWOOD, about 1763, ht. 5¼ in (13.4 cm)
    Victoria and Albert Museum. See pages 35 and 43

8B TEAPOT, decorated with green and yellow glazes and pastoral scenes in relief
    Moulded by GREATBATCH, coloured by WEDGWOOD, about 1763, ht. 4½ in
    (11.2 cm)
    Victoria and Albert Museum. See page 43

and a number would seem to be of Leeds origin (Plate 80B). There is however a large group of them which have a simple fret- or key-pattern moulded border which do not readily fit in with any known factory style and it may be that these are of Greatbatch manufacture.

The following is a list of some of the engraved subjects which occur on this class of creamware:

 1 'The Prodigal Son receives his patrimony'
 2 'The Prodigal Son taking his leave'
 3 'The Prodigal Son in excess' (Plate 36A)
 4 'The Prodigal Son in misery'
 5 'The Prodigal Son returns reclaimed'
 6 'The Prodigal Son feasted on his return'
 7 'The Prodigal Son receives his patrimony' 2nd series
 8 'The Prodigal Son taking his leave' 2nd series
 9 'The Fortune Teller'[1] (Plate 80B)
10 'Juno'
11 'Aurora' (two versions) (Plate 23B)[2]
12 'Captain Cook being directed by Britannia' (Plate 35A)
13 'Admiral Keppel' (Plate 35B)
14 'Man of War in full sail'
15 'A Lady and Gentleman walking in a garden'
16 'Harlequin and Columbine discovered in an arbour'
17 'Twelve Houses of Heaven' (Plate 36B)
18 'The World, with Sun, Moon and Stars'
19 'Cybele'

Since I wrote the above, the site of the Greatbatch works has been discovered. It is situated in the centre of Fenton in the area which must have been known as Lane Delph in the eighteenth century. A great variety of shards were found, some of which bore the impressed mark of William Greatbatch — which consisted of the letters WG in the form of a monogram (Appendix III: mark 39A).

This discovery throws much light on the Greatbatch productions and confirms what has already been said in this section on Greatbatch concerning the various types of ware he produced. There were, however, shards of a

---

pointed out however that in his notebook Whieldon refers to the employment of Daniel's son and as it is known that he employed William Greatbatch, it looks as though Daniel was William's father. A tea-caddy in the Delhom Collection, now at the Mint Museum, North Carolina is inscribed 'Daniel Greatbatch'. The registers also show a William and Mary Greatbatch of Little Fenton, an Isaac and Mary, another Daniel and a Thomas. This last was probably the turner who is said to have invented the engine lathe. During the early part of the nineteenth century a William Greatbatch and an H. Greatbatch exhibited engravings at the Royal Academy.
[1] Usually marked 'Greatbatch' in the print.
[2] The subject of 'Aurora' is also found in enamelled painting only, on teapots of a fine quality creamware which were probably made at Leeds (Plate 80A).

9A TEAPOT, with panels moulded in relief and decorated with coloured glazes
Moulded by GREATBATCH, coloured by WEDGWOOD, about 1763, ht. 4¼ in
(10.7 cm)
Victoria and Albert Museum. See pages 34 and 43
9B TEAPOT, with panels moulded in relief and coloured over in enamels
Probably made by WILLIAM GREATBATCH for WEDGWOOD, about 1764, ht.
5¾ in (14.5 cm). Cf. Plate 9A
Zeitlin Collection. See pages 34 and 50

number of patterns which are unrecorded. This is especially true of moulded border patterns, but among examples of the better known ones we find a variation of the 'feather' border with seven small equally spaced barbs, the end one being larger as usual. The diamond border occurs not only on the usual octagonal plates but also on some with a wavy edge. The shell edge occurs on pearlware with underglaze-blue painting. Of particular interest is a border of the simple fret or key pattern round a teapot cover. There were also specimens of spout (Appendix I, Plate II, fig. 8), flower knob (Appendix I, Plate VII, fig. 1), terminals (Appendix I, Plate IX, fig. 16), handle (Appendix I, Plate IV, fig. 3) and the pierced ball knob. This confirms that the 'Prodigal Son' type of teapot with fret borders or these details was made by Greatbatch.

The creamware generally was of good quality, sometimes very finely crazed. Enamel painting was mostly of floral patterns in red, pink, yellow, green, black and purple, but from the few samples of this so far found it appeared to be somewhat nondescript.

Shards of the earlier wares so far found on the site consisted of tortoiseshell ware in brown and green in the style of Whieldon, wares formed as a basket of fruit, cauliflower ware and pineapple ware. All these were in the biscuit and were also found on the Whieldon site. A shard with the barley-corn pattern was found as well, which no doubt was intended for salt-glazing.

Of the later ware was a whitish creamware and pearlware with underglaze-blue painting of the 'pagoda' pattern. A transfer-printed piece from 'The Prodigal Son in Excess' (Plate 36A, page 87) has recently been found on the site.

Taken as a whole the Greatbatch products were much as one would have expected them to be, but it is very satisfactory to have this confirmed.[1]

---

[1] The above information was made accessible by the kind services of Mr. J. L. Evans of Stoke-on-Trent who discovered the site of the Greatbatch factory in September 1977.

Chapter 3

JOSIAH WEDGWOOD

It has already been stated in the last chapter that in 1754 Josiah Wedgwood, then aged twenty-four, entered into a partnership with Thomas Whieldon. This was the first decisive step in Wedgwood's notable career. The five years he spent with Whieldon may be considered as a period of preparation, when glazes, forms and ideas in general were evolved and crystallized. The wares produced by Wedgwood during this period cannot be differentiated from those of Thomas Whieldon, but it might be remarked that the later wares of this period which seem to have become more and more under the influence of Wedgwood were more completely covered with coloured glazes than the earlier ones, so that for economical reasons a common earthenware body, as Wedgwood called it, was used instead of the finer creamware. These were the fruit and vegetable wares in particular. Wedgwood's experiments took place at Fenton Hall, whereas the main productions of the partnership period were made at Fenton Vivian. Wedgwood severed his partnership with Whieldon in 1759 and started on his own account, first at the Ivy House, Burslem, and then in 1764 at the Brick House, Burslem, known later as the Bell Works.

The true Wedgwood creamware may be said to have been first produced at the Ivy House in 1760 or the early part of 1761. At first it was of a rich buff colour covered with a glaze having a yellowish-green tinge which was inclined to craze, and there is no doubt that Wedgwood's chief efforts at this time were directed towards producing a creamware which would not only be more refined in body, glaze, design and finish but would also be paler in colour. A teapot of the Ivy House period is illustrated (Plate 12A). As already stated in the last chapter, Wedgwood, on leaving Whieldon, entered into an agreement with William Greatbatch who was to supply him with teapots in the white ready for glazing; some fine creamware covered with a rich green glaze, sometimes with sprigs in relief touched with gold or pricked with a pointed tool to form dots, is of this period (Plate 8A). Teapots moulded with designs in relief and others in the form of fruits and vegetables, such as the melon and cauliflower ware, continued to be made (Plates 7B, 8B and 9A).

Between 1763 and 1767 Wedgwood made a great many changes not only in the body and glaze of the creamware but also in the methods of its manufacture. Eliza Meteyard in her *Life of Wedgwood* tells how he improved the kilns as well as every tool, instrument and apparatus at the factory, sometimes replacing them with new types of his own invention. The most important change, however, as already stated in the Introduction, was the incorporation of Cornish china-clay and -stone into both body and glaze. This not only produced a much paler creamware but also gave it a lightness and brilliance which was wholly new.

The following letter written by Wedgwood in 1768 to his London office shows that having abandoned the deep cream-colour he was not in a position to resort to it again, at this time at any rate:

> With respect to the colour of my ware, I endeavour to make it as pale as possible to continue it cream-colour and find my customers in general, though not every individual of them, think the alteration I have made in that respect a great improvement, but it is impossible that any one colour, even though it were to come down from Heaven, should please every taste, and I cannot regularly make two cream-colours, a deep and a light shade, without having two works for that purpose.

It follows that since Wedgwood in 1768 was unable to make both the deep and the pale coloured creamware at the same time, the smaller factories were still less able to do so. This fact is a valuable aid to the identification and dating of early creamware. Thus the Wedgwood creamware of from 1763 to 1770 was much paler in colour than the Yorkshire of the corresponding period. It was also paler than the Daniels' creamware of 1775, as is evidenced by a cake-basket in the British Museum with the incised signature and date 'John Daniel, 1775' (see Appendix III:101).

Glazes

The glaze on the earliest marked pieces of Wedgwood's creamware, as already stated, was strongly tinged with yellowish-green, and sometimes showed considerable crazing. With the refining of the body, however, a finer glaze was introduced which though also greenish, appeared much paler, as it was more thinly and evenly applied, with the consequent elimination of crazing. This was a glaze of great beauty which when applied to the creamware body seemed to glow with life. It was usually of sufficient strength of colour to give the ware a slight greenish tinge. This is particularly apparent on the inside of teapots, which are greener than those of Leeds manufacture. After about 1763 crazing on Wedgwood's creamware was rare, and except for some whitish creamware of a much later date which was covered with a blue-green glaze, and the pearlware[1] which was coated with a sufficient quantity of bluish glaze to counteract the cream colour of the body, the creamware continued to be coated

[1] Wedgwood introduced his pearlware in 1779.

10   COFFEE-POT, deep cream, transfer-printed in red at LIVERPOOL. 'Tea Party' on
      reverse
      WEDGWOOD, about 1763, ht. 8¾ in (22.25 cm)
      Formerly Towner Collection. See pages 64 and 172

with the yellow-green glaze, which though remaining the same tint became
consistently paler till by the end of the century it was almost colourless. The
blue glaze of Wedgwood's pearlware has a slightly greenish tinge which is
entirely absent in the Leeds pearlware. Probably the most distinctive
characteristic of the later Wedgwood glazes is their thin and even application,
which eventually tended to produce an almost mechanical uniformity of
surface, and consequent lack of life.

Forms and Details

Wedgwood, while preserving a globular form for his teapots, modified it by compressing the top and sides. This shape which would appear to have been derived from his melon teapots (Plate 7B) was used for the great majority of his creamware teapots throughout the eighteenth century, but was quickly copied by other potters. The adoption of Wedgwood forms by other Staffordshire potters was probably encouraged by Josiah himself, as he formed stocks of ware made by a number of other potteries, which he referred to in a letter as 'banks', from which he could make up his crates when he himself was unable to meet all the orders for creamware which he received. This arrangement was mutual. Letters and bills from Anne Warburton and Sons, the Daniels and other potters, dating from 1762 to 1799 and now in the Keele University Library, refer to ware sold to, or bought from, Josiah Wedgwood. A letter quoted by Miss Meteyard shows Josiah's annoyance at the inability of Thomas Byerley, Wedgwood's nephew and London representative, to distinguish between the Wedgwood creamware and that of the 'banks' (Vol. I, p. 357).[1]

It is surprising how rarely Wedgwood used the crabstock spout, handle and knob for his early teapots, considering how much it was used by other potters of the 1750s and 60s including Thomas Whieldon both for saltglaze and the deep cream-coloured creamware (Appendix I, Plate I: 1, and Plate IV: 1). One finds them on some of the apple and pear teapots of the partnership period and then they seem to have been totally discarded in favour of new designs—the wrapped-leaf spout, the shell spout, and above all the cauliflower spout (Appendix I, Plate III: 1, Plate II: 3 and 1). All these we find on Wedgwood's early colour-glazed ware as well as on creamware of the Burslem period and the two last well into the Etruria period as well. Probably ninety per cent of Wedgwood's eighteenth-century teapots have cauliflower spouts. The accompanying handles were two varieties of scroll in the Burslem period (Appendix I, Plate IV: 3 and 3A) and the scale and double handle in the Etruria period (Appendix I, Plate V: 1 and 3). Most Wedgwood teapots have a pierced bulbous knob with a short finial (Appendix I, Plate VIII: 3), but a flower knob, almost invariably of one type, is found in conjunction with the double handle (Appendix I, Plate VII: 8). A second pattern of flower knob, based on the rose, was occasionally used on some types of ware (Appendix I, Plate VII: 9) (Plate 26B). Wedgwood cake-baskets with pierced sides etc. having a Leeds type flower knob are late reproductions usually of the twentieth century.

Enamelling

The correspondence between Wedgwood and the Warburtons (see page 32) only relates to sales of creamware to each other and no mention is made of enamelling.

The first reference to any enamelling in the Wedgwood correspondence is

---

[1] For further notes on the forms and details of Wedgwood's creamware see Appendix I.

IIA   SUGAR-BOWL, deep cream, transfer-printed in red at LIVERPOOL
      WEDGWOOD, about 1763, diam. 4¾ in (12 cm)
      TEAPOT, paler cream, transfer-printed in black at LIVERPOOL
      WEDGWOOD, about 1765, ht. 5¾ in (14.5 cm)
      Victoria and Albert Museum. See pages 64 and 172

IIB   TEAPOT, paler cream, transfer-printed in black at LIVERPOOL
      WEDGWOOD, about 1764, ht. 7 in (17.75 cm)
      British Museum. See pages 64 and 172

12A   TEAPOT, painted with thick enamel in a saltglaze style in pink, green, yellow, blue and black
      WEDGWOOD, about 1762, ht. 4 in (10.2 cm)
      Towner Collection. See pages 32, 43 and 50
12B   TEAPOT, painted in purple monochrome
      WEDGWOOD, about 1765, ht. 4¾ in (12 cm)
      Towner Collection

13A SWEETMEAT-DISH, deep cream enamelled in purple monochrome. Marks
'WEDGWOOD' impressed and 'G' painted in purple
WEDGWOOD, about 1765, length $7\frac{3}{4}$ in (19.75 cm)
Victoria and Albert Museum. See pages 58 and 223
13B PLATE, deep cream, enamelled in black and yellow probably by J. BAKEWELL.
Impressed workman's mark 74
WEDGWOOD, about 1765, diam. $8\frac{1}{2}$ in (21.5 cm)
Towner Collection. See page 58

contained in the letter quoted on page 36, written by William Greatbatch to
Wedgwood on 12 July 1763, in which Mr. Courzen's painting shop is
mentioned. It may be that the enamelling on teapots of the Chinese hexagonal
pattern (Plate 9B) or on teapots which were clearly enamelled by a saltglaze
decorator, was his work (Plate 12A). A letter[1] dated 11 March 1763, shows that
Wedgwood had already entered into business negotiations with Robinson and
Rhodes, enamellers of Leeds, who at that time were buying his ware and had
supplied him with the name of an engraver to cut the seals or brass stamps for
his applied ornaments. The following order is enclosed in this letter:

1 doz. flowered 18^s[2] teapotts mellon colour
1 „   18^s do $\frac{1}{2}$ doz. 24^s
1 „   24^s do. —pine apple shape.
4 green oval fruit basketts and Dishes the basketts about 7$\frac{1}{2}$ inches broad.
12 dry red teapotts some of them with Crab tree spouts.
1 doz. Teapotts, a few of them 24^s of your neatest and newest fashioned sort.
     In sending the above mentioned soon you'll oblige us much and we shall
want many more of them.
                              for Partner and Self
                              Yr most humble Servt. Dav^d. Rhodes.

On 2 May 1763 Rhodes was supplying Wedgwood with copper scales for his
green glaze.
     The following letters to Wedgwood perhaps denote the beginning of actual
work by Rhodes on Wedgwood's creamware:

                              Leeds 21st November. 1764.
     I received your Favour, and shall be glad to serve you in anything I can
do. I have burnt Gold on China often and am certain I can do it on your
ware; . . .
     My partner has turned over the business to me since March last and works
for me at it.
                              Sr. Your most humble Servt.
                              Dav^d. Rhodes.

                              Leeds. Dec. 13. 1764.
     Desire you would send me the Cream Coloured teapotts immediately if
you have them.—
                              Dav^d. Rhodes.

Some rare very early Wedgwood teapots which would seem to date from
about 1764 are painted by Rhodes in black and red. One such depicts a

[1] This and all other letters relating to Wedgwood and quoted in this book are from the
Wedgwood correspondence at the Keele University Library.
[2] 18^s, 24^s, etc., refer to sizes.

14A   DISH, painted in purple by J. BAKEWELL. Mark 'J.B.' in monogram painted in
      purple
      WEDGWOOD, about 1765, length 11¾ in (30 cm)
      Towner Collection. See page 58

14B   TEACUP and SAUCER, deep cream painted in green monochrome
      WEDGWOOD, about 1770, ht. of cup 1¾ in (4.5 cm), diam. of saucer 4¾ in (12 cm)
      Formerly Towner Collection

musician seated on a well playing an oboe, while a plaintive dog rests one paw on his master's knee. This is almost certainly one of the 'Cream Coloured teapotts' which Wedgwood sent to Leeds for Rhodes, or one of his enamellers, to decorate (Plate 15B).

Unfortunately there are no further records of Rhodes till 24 March 1768 when Wedgwood wrote to Bentley telling him that he had acquired the lease of a warehouse in St. Martin's Lane and continues:

> I have already agreed with one very useful Tenant A Master Enameler and China piecer. . . . I have long had connections with this Man, who is sober and steady, he is just come out of Yorkshire to settle here. . . . he paints flowers and Landskips very prettily, prepares a pretty good powder gold, and has a tolerable notion of Colours. He has an Apprentice and another hand, I have set him to work upon Table and desert ware, and shall get his rooms ready in St. Martin's Lane immediately.

On 20 June 1768, Wedgwood writes to Mr. Cox, Queen's Arms, London, as follows:

> I have yours today of ye 18 and have one from Mr Rhodes acquainting me he has got a partner[1] who has Enam.ᵈ at Paris and does it with great Elegance and wants to begin upon some small plates immediately wch. you'l please to furnish them with I shall write to Mr. Rhodes this post.
>
> Yr. frd. and Serᵗ. J.W.

Bills from Rhodes dating from 27 December 1768 till 23 December 1769 amounting to £178.10.1 are headed 'Ware of Mr. Josiah Wedgwood to be enamelled at D. Rhodes & Co'.

There are numerous letters in the correspondence showing how highly Wedgwood esteemed Rhodes as an enameller:

> 19 Nov. 1769. To Thos. Bentley
> I have reserved my house at Burslem for Mr. Rhodes and his Men, it is quite ready for him and when he comes you shall have Mr. Bakewell, but we must have somebody here to vein and finish the vases. . . .

Types of painting mentioned in the letters as being done by Rhodes are: flowers, landscapes, figures, husks, table-plate with 'Purple and Gold', as well as veining (marbling) and painting on Etruscan Vases.

---

[1] David Rhodes entered into partnership with William Hopkins Craft. Receipts, at the Keele University Library, signed by Rhodes and Craft cover the years 1769 and 1770, after which the partnership was probably dissolved. Four signed and dated examples of William Craft's enamelling on copper are at the British Museum. His work on Wedgwood's ware however almost certainly consisted of the Etruscan figures in red on black basaltes.

15A TEAPOT, pale cream, enamelled in red, black, purple, green and yellow by D.
RHODES AND CO.
WEDGWOOD, about 1768, ht. 4¾ in (12 cm) (The cover is a replacement of Leeds
manufacture)
Victoria and Albert Museum. See page 54

15B TEAPOT, deep cream, enamelled at Leeds in red and black by ROBINSON and
RHODES
WEDGWOOD, about 1764, ht. 5½ in (14 cm)
Byron Born Collection. See page 52

To Thos. Bentley, Queen's Arms, Newport Street.

10 Jan. 1770

... If I had Mr. Rhodes here you shod. soon have some Etruscan Vases painted at Etruria, but I cannot attempt anything farther without such assistance. ... When does Mr. Rhodes intend to be here. ...

J.W.

Rhodes never went.

The teapot at the Victoria and Albert Museum having a figure in a landscape can be identified as the work of Rhodes (Plate 15A). The treatment of details, such as the crossed tree and foliage, is identical with Leeds saltglaze and creamware painting. On the reverse of this same teapot is some fine flower painting, also similar in treatment to some done at Leeds. (The cover to the teapot (Plate 15A) was made at the Leeds Pottery and is a replacement.) Some pieces of Wedgwood's creamware are enamelled in the same style, but show a different treatment of foliage and may therefore have been done by one of Rhodes' assistants.[1] This treatment of foliage occurs on a teapot in the Castle Museum, Norwich, which has a standing figure enamelled on one side and is inscribed 'Success to Sir Charles Holte Esq' (Plate 17A). Sir Charles Holte was a contestant at Birmingham for the parliamentary election of 1774, so that the teapot can be dated precisely. Other examples of Rhodes's figure painting are illustrated on Colour Plate B and Plate 16B.

In April 1773, Wedgwood writes, 'I think Mr. Rhodes cannot be better employ'd than in painting Landskips.' The teapot with a landscape illustrated (Plate 16A), may date from about this time.

The colours used by Rhodes for figures, flowers and landscapes on Wedgwood creamware are red, black, green, rosy purple and yellow (Colour Plate B). During the time that Rhodes was at Leeds the palette he then used was mostly confined to red and black though he sometimes introduced touches of green, rosy purple, yellow and other colours.

Among other enamelled designs found on Wedgwood's creamware we may first mention the very delightful and original banded and diapered patterns (Plate 19). These also are painted in red, black, rosy purple, green and yellow, and occur not only on Wedgwood creamware but also on that of the Leeds Pottery. On some pieces, this type of decoration is combined with flower painting in the style of Rhodes. It seems to be certain therefore that he was their author (Plate 17B).

A slightly different type of flower painting occurs on Wedgwood creamware, in which a thick opaque rosy pink is conspicuous, other colours being red, green, blue, black and yellow (Plate 18A). Teapots enamelled by Rhodes in all the above styles are sometimes found with rose-coloured handles and spouts. Wedgwood teapots with this last style of painting are a deeper cream than the

---

[1] It would appear that a single piece of decoration was often the work of more than one enameller.

16A TEAPOT, pale cream, enamelled in red, black, purple, green and yellow by D. RHODES AND CO. Mark 'Wedgwood' impressed
WEDGWOOD, about 1774, ht. $4\frac{1}{2}$ in (11.2 cm)
Zeitlin Collection. See pages 54 and 223

16B TEAPOT, pale cream, enamelled in red, black, purple, green and yellow by D. RHODES AND CO.
WEDGWOOD, about 1766, ht. $5\frac{1}{2}$ in (14 cm)
Leeds Art Galleries. See pages 35 and 54

17A   TEAPOT, pale cream, enamelled in red, black, purple, green and yellow by D. RHODES AND Co. Inscribed on the reverse 'Success to Sir Charles Holte Esq' WEDGWOOD, 1774, ht. 5½ in (14 cm)
Norwich Castle Museum. See page 54

17B   TEAPOT, pale cream, enamelled in red, black, purple, green, yellow and pink by D. RHODES AND Co.
WEDGWOOD, about 1768, ht. 4¾ in (12 cm)
Trustees of T. M. Ragg. See page 54

18A TEAPOT, deep cream enamelled in red, black, blue, yellow, pink and green by D.
     RHODES AND CO.
     WEDGWOOD, about 1770, ht. 6 in (15.2 cm)
     Norwich Castle Museum. See page 54
18B TEAPOT, pale cream, enamelled in red, black, purple, blue, green and yellow.
     Impressed mark 'Wedgwood'
     ETRURIA, about 1775, ht. 4½ in (11.5 cm)
     Zeitlin Collection. See pages 58 and 223

enamelled teapots already mentioned and are earlier in date. An enameller's mark of three green spots arranged in the form of a triangle sometimes occurs on teapots painted both in this and the banded style already mentioned.

Another type of flower painting somewhat similar to the last, but in which the rosy pink is replaced by a rosy purple (Plate 18B), is less vigorous and of a slightly different technique, and the teapots on which it is found would appear to have been made after 1770. This enamelling may also be by one of Rhodes's enamellers.

In a letter from Josiah Wedgwood to Thomas Bentley dated 23 May 1770, he says: 'Bakewell has set his mind to be a good enamel Painter and really improves much both in flowers and in Copying figures.'

Some freely-painted naturalistic flowers in purple or crimson monochrome occur on dessert-services, whose borders usually have a fringe or 'feathered' edging of the same colour (Plate 13A). They are sometimes marked underneath in enamel with the letters 'B', 'D' or 'G', which probably stand for James Bakewell, Catharine Dent and Thomas Green, whose names appear on a Wedgwood account for enamelling dated October 1770. Painting of a similar nature was done in black and yellow (Plate 13B). This and the purple enamelling marked with the letter 'B' or 'J.B.' in monogram (Plate 14A) were undoubtedly painted by James Bakewell, as the following letter shows:

> 22 July, 1770 Josiah Wedgwood to Thos. Bentley.
> . . . If Mr. Rhodes stays with you I cannot attempt any of these things. . . . James Bakewell is not, nor ever will be able to take enough of the care and management of these matters off my hands for me to ingage deeply in them. With him, all I can think of undertaking will be Bronzeing and the black and yellow, and purple enamelling and this not to any extent.

The flower painting by Bakewell and his enamellers would have been done at Burslem.

Some enamelling was done, to Wedgwood's order, by Sadler and Green of Liverpool. Included in this was enamelling with transparent washes of green applied over black transfer-prints of sea shells and flowers (Plate 25). Thus we read of '$12\frac{3}{4}$ Doz. small Plates green shell @ 4/6 £2.17.$4\frac{1}{2}$' in a bill sent to Wedgwood from Guy Green. Green also enamelled border edges, etc.

> Liverpool. Sept. 2. 1777.
>
> To Mr. Josiah Wedgwood,
> Sir,
>
> By Dan Morris was sent $4\frac{1}{2}$ doz. Dessert Plates Purple edge. My enamellers were about one day in doing a Dozen of them for which they charged me 2/6—I shall be glad to know what you pay as I cannot be persuaded but they must be done a good deal cheaper. I am endeavouring to get the obstacles of their heavy charges removed, by bringing forwards some boys and girls who are now under the care of an Enameller for that purpose.
>
> Yours etc.   Guy Green.

19 COFFEE-POT, pale cream, enamelled in red, black, purple, green and yellow by
D. RHODES AND CO.
WEDGWOOD, about 1775, ht. 10 in (25.5 cm)
Trustees of T. M. Ragg. See pages 54 and 224

The edging of Wedgwood's transfer-printed ware in a single enamel colour
had been done by Sadler and Green for a long time before the above letter was
written, but this letter clearly indicates something more ambitious. For
although edging only is mentioned, it would not be likely that Green's
enamellers would take a whole day to edge twelve plates. The letter may refer
to Wedgwood purple-edged dessert-plates with finely-painted flowers in the

centre enamelled in a number of other colours. Similar plates but without the flower painting are more commonly found.

Phillips and Greaves, enamellers at Stoke, were responsible for some unidentified painting in blue enamel on Wedgwood's creamware about the year 1764.

In 1765, Wedgwood received an order for a creamware tea and coffee service from Queen Charlotte, which is described in a letter written by Josiah to John Wedgwood:

> The order came from Miss Deborah, alias Deb Chetwynd, Sempstress and Laundress to the Queen, to Mr. Smallwood of Newcastle, who bro[t] it to me (I believe because nobody else wo[d] undertake it), & is as follows: 'A complete sett of tea things, with a gold ground and raised flowers upon it in green, in the same manner of the green flowers that are raised upon the *mehons*, so it is wrote, but I suppose it sho[d] be *melons*—The articles are 12 cups for Tea, & 12 saucers, a slop basin, sugar dish wth cover and stand— Teapot & stand, spoon trea—Coffeepot, 12 Coffeecups, 6 p[r] of hand candlesticks & six melons with leaves, 6 green fruit baskets, and stands edged with gold.'

This service, of which not a single specimen is known today, was delivered towards the end of the year 1765, and led to further orders from the royal family. The Queen's continued patronage prompted Wedgwood to adopt the name 'Queen's ware' for his creamware. This title for creamware was afterwards adopted by many other potters, but was applied to the pale coloured creamware only.

Another service of far greater magnitude was made for Catherine II of Russia in 1774. It was in fact a complete table-service for fifty persons and originally consisted of 952 pieces which included soup-tureens, compotiers, vegetable-dishes with covers, sauce-tureens, monteiths, butter-boats, ladles, ice-pails, fruit-bowls, baskets, salvers, cream-pots, saucers with handles, soup-plates, bread-plates, dinner-plates, dessert-plates and dishes of various shapes and sizes. Each piece was painted with different topographical views of Great Britain. Both these and the oak-leaf border that surrounds them are painted in sepia monochrome surmounted by a green frog in a shield (Plate 20B). A few trial pieces painted in natural colours and without the frog are on the whole more pleasing.

The landscapes were painted by James Bakewell,[1] Mrs. Wilcox and Ralph Unwin from drawings by a number of artists who toured the country making them. Many of the scenes drawn were suggested by Wedgwood himself. A number of enamellers were employed to paint the borders and the whole of the decorative work was executed at Chelsea under the direction of David Rhodes.

---

[1] Chelsea ratebooks show that Bakewell was living in Lordship Yard, Chelsea from the second half of 1773 till the second half of 1774.

20A PLATE, transfer-printed in red at LIVERPOOL with the fable of 'The Fox and the Goat'. Festoons and rim painted in green. Impressed mark 'WEDGWOOD' WEDGWOOD (BURSLEM), about 1770, diam. 10 in (25.5 cm)
Victoria and Albert Museum

20B PLATE, pale cream, painted in dark sepia, the frog in green, from the service made for Catherine II of Russia. Impressed mark 'WEDGWOOD' WEDGWOOD, 1774, diam. $9\frac{1}{2}$ in (24.2 cm)
Victoria and Albert Museum. See page 60

21A   SAUCEBOAT, deep cream, transfer-printed in purple at LIVERPOOL
       WEDGWOOD (BURSLEM), about 1770, length 6½ in (16.5 cm)
       Victoria and Albert Museum. See pages 64 and 172
21B   PLATE, deep cream, transfer-printed in red at LIVERPOOL
       WEDGWOOD (BURSLEM), about 1770, diam. 9¼ in (24.2 cm)
       Formerly Towner Collection. See pages 64 and 172

22A BOWL, pale cream, transfer-printed in black at LIVERPOOL by Sadler and
Green. Impressed mark 'WEDGWOOD'
WEDGWOOD, about 1772, diam. 8 in (20.3 cm)
Formerly Towner Collection. See pages 64, 172 and 223

22B TEAPOT, pale cream, transfer-printed in black. Mark 'Green Liverpool' in the
print, an incised cross underneath
WEDGWOOD, about 1775, ht. 4¾ in (12 cm)
Formerly Towner Collection. See pages 64 and 172

Several pieces of the finished service made their way back to this country or perhaps were never sent and, however we may judge it from an artistic point of view, the fact that Wedgwood was able to place a creamware service of such magnitude on the dining-table of the Empress Catherine II of Russia was an undoubted triumph.

Of considerable importance was Wedgwood's introduction of creamware decorated with enamelled formal border patterns (Plate 28B). These prim little designs have an undoubted charm and were painted under the supervision of David Rhodes at Little China Row, Chelsea,[1] from which address on the 4 May 1770, he was advertising for additional hands to help with the enamelling. This is the type of enamelling most commonly found on Wedgwood's creamware made after 1770, and by reason of its suitability to its purpose has been deservedly popular ever since its first introduction. Not only were the creamware shapes of this ware copied by other potters, but the border patterns were reproduced by a number of English and Continental creamware factories. The Wedgwood ware of this type is usually marked.

Transfer-printing

In 1761 Wedgwood entered into negotiations with John Sadler of Liverpool to print on his creamware from engraved plates. Although transfer-printing had previously been employed on enamels, tiles, porcelain and possibly saltglaze, this may be said to be the beginning of transfer-printing as a means of decorating creamware. John Sadler has left an account of his work for Wedgwood in his notebook now at the Liverpool Public Library and this has been largely drawn upon by E. Stanley Price in his book entitled *John Sadler, a Liverpool Pottery Printer*.

Of importance is a statement by Sadler in a letter to Wedgwood dated 11 October 1763: 'you may rest assured we never printed a piece for any person but yourself', and generally speaking we can say that Wedgwood's creamware was printed by Sadler and Green and that Sadler and Green's printing on creamware was done for Wedgwood with very few exceptions.

The first printing on Wedgwood's deep cream-coloured ware was either in black or red and included a great variety of subjects. Examples of early printing by Sadler on Wedgwood creamware are illustrated on Plates 10, 11A and 11B. Later examples by Sadler and Green will be found on Plates 21A, B, 22A, B, 23A and 25. The Wesley teapot on Plate 22B is signed 'Green, Liverpool' in the print.

The red printing was a fairly deep, dull red, unlike the orange red of Leeds. On the early Wedgwood creamware the colour of the printing was slightly influenced by the colour of the glaze. Thus the black tended to appear brownish and the red slightly more orange than on the later wares. Purple printing was introduced in 1770 and varied between a rich plum and purplish

---

[1] Chelsea ratebooks show that Rhodes occupied premises in Little Cheyne Row from 1769 to 1775, after which his house is shown as empty. This house, formerly No. 2 Little Cheyne Row, is now 26 Upper Cheyne Row.

A   TEAPOT, decorated with coloured glazes
WHIELDON, about 1750, ht. 4¾ in (12.1 cm)
Victoria and Albert Museum. See page 28

B   MUG, enamelled by D. RHODES AND CO.
WEDGWOOD, about 1770, ht. 5 in (12.7 cm)
Zeitlin Collection. See page 54

23A   TEAPOT, pale cream, transfer-printed in black at LIVERPOOL. Impressed mark
       'WEDGWOOD'
       ETRURIA, about 1780, ht. 5½ in (14 cm)
       Fitzwilliam Museum, Cambridge. See pages 64 and 172
23B   TEAPOT, pale cream, transfer-printed in black from an engraving by W.
       GREATBATCH and enamelled in red, black, green, rose and yellow
       WEDGWOOD, about 1775, ht. 5 in (12.2 cm)
       Victoria and Albert Museum. See pages 38, 40, 67 and 70

24   COVERED JUG, pale cream, transfer-printed in deep red. Impressed mark
'Wedgwood'
ETRURIA, about 1775, ht. 5¾ in (14.6 cm)
Formerly Towner Collection. See pages 223, 224

grey. Landscapes in purple were among the most pleasing of all Wedgwood's
transfer-printed creamware.

Portrait subjects include Lord Bute; Marquis of Granby; John Wilkes;
King George III; Queen Charlotte; William Pitt; the King of Prussia;
Admiral Rodney; John Wesley, etc.

Armorial subjects include The Masons' Arms, The Society of Bucks, Anti-
Gallican Society. Amongst the many figure subjects are 'The Haymakers',

25 COFFEE-POT, very pale cream, transfer-printed in black and enamelled over in two shades of green; traces of gilding. Decorated by GREEN, LIVERPOOL. Impressed mark 'WEDGWOOD'
ETRURIA, about 1777, ht. 8½ in (21.5 cm)
Formerly Towner Collection. See pages 58, 64 and 223

'Harvest Home', 'Tithe Pig', 'Triple Plea', 'Tea Party', 'Harlequinade', fables, exotic birds, shepherd, etc. There are a number of versions of most of these.

Landscapes occur either in black, red or purple. The borders are usually decorated with birds or flowers.

In addition to the subjects already mentioned, some Wedgwood teapots have 'Aurora' printed on them on one side, and on the reverse 'The Twelve Houses of Heaven'. These prints, which are washed over in enamel colours,

26A   COFFEE-CUP and SAUCER, shell moulding, gilded decoration. Impressed mark
      'Wedgwood'
      WEDGWOOD, about 1770, ht. of cup $2\frac{1}{4}$ in (5.7 cm), diam. of saucer $4\frac{3}{4}$ in (12 cm)
      Towner Collection. See page 223

26B   BUTTER-DISH, pale cream, uncoloured. Mark 'WEDGWOOD' impressed
      ETRURIA, about 1780, ht. $3\frac{1}{2}$ in (9 cm), diam. $5\frac{3}{4}$ in (14.6 cm)
      Victoria and Albert Museum. See page 46

27   VASE, deep cream, mottled with coloured glazes of blue and brown to simulate
      granite. Black basalt base impressed 'WEDGWOOD AND BENTLEY ETRURIA'
      ETRURIA, about 1773, ht. 12¾ in (32.5 cm)
      Victoria and Albert Museum. See page 70

were engraved by William Greatbatch as previously explained in Chapter 2 (Plate 23B).

Classical Influence and Etruria

Wedgwood's creamware vases date from the time when he came under the influence of the Adam brothers who incorporated urn-shaped vases of agate, bluejohn and other semi-precious stones into their decorative schemes. Wedgwood's first vases were of uncoloured creamware of a fairly deep cream-colour with moulded reliefs, sometimes with engine turning and touched with gold, and can be dated from about 1764. From Wedgwood's letters to Thomas Bentley in 1765 it would appear that some of these were transfer-printed, but the present author has no knowledge of any such pieces.

As a result of Wedgwood's increasing interest in the antique we find him hunting for designs and preparing models of a more classical form. Writing to Bentley in May 1767 and again in June of that year he says 'Vases sell', 'I am picking up every design and improvement for vase work', and 'I am preparing designs, models, moulds, clays, colours etc. for the vase work'. Thus a scholarly approach was given to Wedgwood's creamware, which we find influenced the useful wares as well. Designs were now prepared on paper from which to work. Some of these were by well-known artists such as Flaxman, the sculptor, who in 1775 sent Wedgwood a bill for designing vases amongst other things.

The year 1769 was an important one in the history of the Wedgwood factory, for in August of that year Thomas Bentley became Wedgwood's partner to be in charge of the ornamental wares at the London showrooms, a position he was to occupy till his death in 1780; secondly, it was in 1769 that the Wedgwood works at Etruria were opened. The very name 'Etruria' was an indication of the nature of the wares to be produced there, and consequently we find a great deal of concentration being centred on vases in various materials. The creamware vases of the Wedgwood and Bentley period (1769–80) were very different from the creamware vases of a few years earlier. Wedgwood had developed a more classical form and was able to use a much more refined creamware for them. They were now decorated in underglaze colours, a direct development from his tortoiseshell and other colour-glazed wares of the Whieldon period, but they were now intended to simulate semi-precious stones. Wedgwood referred to them as 'blue pebble vases' (Plate 27). They usually possessed handles, swags and masks of plain moulded creamware covered with gilding which in many cases has now worn off. They were mounted on white jasper or black basalt bases. These last usually bore the circular Wedgwood and Bentley impressed mark. It is a matter of some wonder as to the complete transformation of creamware in appearance, status and function within a matter of ten years from the time Wedgwood left Whieldon. Today we may not all like the rigid classical forms of the vases, but in their time they were very much in vogue and were sought after as being equally effective and less costly than the stone vases they imitated. Meanwhile the useful wares continued to be made at Burslem until

28A   JELLY-MOULD and COVER, enamelled in polychrome colours. Impressed mark
       'WEDGWOOD'
       ETRURIA, about 1780, ht. 5 in (12.7 cm), cover ht. 5⅞ in (15 cm)
       Victoria and Albert Museum
28B   TUREEN, pale cream, enamelled in brown, green and purple, enamelled
       inscription added in Holland. Mark 'WEDGWOOD' impressed
       ETRURIA, about 1790, diam. 12 in (30.5 cm)
       Victoria and Albert Museum. See page 64

1773 when the Bell Works were sold and all the apparatus and materials were conveyed to Etruria.

The Pattern Books

Wedgwood issued a number of pattern books, which include catalogues of creamware as well as catalogues of ornamental ware. For notes on those relating to creamware, see Appendix II, pages 215–16.

Figures

Wedgwood himself does not appear to have made any figures in creamware or pearlware, but presumably to meet specific orders he seems to have had a limited number made by the Wood family at Burslem and there impressed with the word 'WEDGWOOD'. The one most commonly found consists of a woman holding a baby and two children. On the front of the base of this figure, the word 'Charity' is impressed and the word 'WEDGWOOD' is impressed at the back. This figure, the modelling of which is typical of the Ralph Woods, is sometimes found decorated with their coloured glazes, but the enamelled creamware version may have been cast and decorated by Enoch Wood. A large enamelled creamware bust of a woman, at the Victoria and Albert Museum, has the word 'Sadness' impressed on the front of its base and the word 'WEDGWOOD' at the back (see Appendix III:50). This figure is undoubtedly the work of Enoch Wood.

Marks

Prior to 1772 much of Wedgwood's creamware was unmarked, but at this date he wrote to Thomas Bentley proposing that all his ware should be marked. Even after this, however, a great many pieces seem to have been sent out of the factory unstamped. The Wedgwood factory mark on creamware consisted of the word 'WEDGWOOD' impressed on the ware. This and other Wedgwood marks are discussed and illustrated in Appendix III.

Chapter 4

LATER STAFFORDSHIRE POTTERS

The Wedgwood factory at Etruria gave the lead to a number of smaller factories in Staffordshire, some of which produced creamware of a very high order. These factories have sometimes been styled plagiarists; but this is doing them an injustice. The creamware produced by them often shows distinctly individual trends and characteristics, and seldom fell to the level of slavish imitation. During the last quarter of the eighteenth century the creamware was to a great extent supplanted in Staffordshire by a pearlware and later a white ware decorated with transfer-prints in underglaze blue. By about 1820 the manufacture of the blue-printed ware had spread to Yorkshire and elsewhere, and its output at that time far exceeded that of any other class of ware.

NEALE AND CO. OF HANLEY

The creamware made by this pottery seems to have been largely overlooked by collectors and others. In quality of body, glaze and workmanship, it often equals the finest productions of the Leeds and Wedgwood factories. It was founded about 1680 by John Palmer, who was one of the pioneers of white salt-glazed stoneware in this country. He was succeeded by his son or grandson Humphrey Palmer who was probably a saltglaze potter too but was better known for his later productions of 'black basalt' and 'jasperware' in the style of Wedgwood. John Neale became his partner in 1776. Humphrey Palmer died in 1778 and Robert Wilson was thereupon engaged by Neale as manager. It seems to have been Wilson who was largely responsible for the beautiful creamware produced by the firm. In 1786 Wilson became a partner.

The creamware produced by Neale and Co. can often be distinguished from that of the Leeds and Wedgwood factories by its peculiar freshness of colour and neatness of execution. This is no doubt partly due to the glaze, which is usually free from all crazing and of a soft pea-green colour of a brighter tint than Wedgwood's glaze. The creamware dessert-services made by Neale and Co. are often of the basket-work pattern with looped borders painted with 'feathered' edging in cobalt blue, emerald green or sepia enamel colours. Such services usually include a large globular covered cream-bowl on a pedestal foot with pierced sides and surmounted by a knob in the form of a pineapple. Other creamware dessert-services are beautifully enamelled with plants copied from herbals with the names of the plants painted on the underside of each piece. Dessert-services of this kind were made by the Swansea, Leeds, Wedgwood, Don, Castleford and other factories during the late eighteenth and early nineteenth centuries, but perhaps the finest were made by Neale. These sometimes bear the impressed mark 'NEALE & BAILEY' (Appendix III: 106). Bailey was a partner from 1780. Other types of creamware include fern-pots and stands. These were square-sided, with intertwined snake handles and were either painted with underglaze green or with flowers in enamel colours. There were also sauce-boats formed like a fish, for fish-sauce, and melon-shaped tureens, sometimes painted with blue 'feathered' edging. Much of the Neale creamware was transfer-printed. This may have been done at the factory. Conspicuous is some brilliant rosy purple printing of shells, also some good landscapes and figure subjects in the same colour. Plates with ships transfer-printed in black and coloured over with enamels sometimes bear the impressed mark 'NEALE & CO.' (Appendix III: 102 and 103).[1]

The factory also made an excellent pearlware with a fine blue-tinted glaze of sufficient depth to give the ware a slightly bluish cast. But it is perhaps best known for its beautiful creamware figures in the neoclassical style of the period, such as the set of 'Seasons' at the Fitzwilliam Museum, Cambridge (Plate 29A and B). With their good modelling, neatness of execution and cleanness of appearance, they are among the most charming creamware figures ever made. There are also some excellent figures in pearlware.

In 1802 David Wilson succeeded to the firm which later traded under the name D. Wilson and Sons. For notes and illustrations of the different marks used by this factory, see Appendix III: 102 to 109.

JOHN TURNER OF LANE END

John Turner, born in 1738, began by making saltglaze at Stoke. He moved to Lane End in 1759 and became one of the most gifted and capable potters of his time, producing a very great variety of wares which included some excellent creamware and pearlware. Much of Turner's creamware was very similar both in body and glaze to that of the Leeds Pottery and consequently differed from the Wedgwood creamware in the same respects. The usual colour of the glaze was primrose yellow. Unlike the Leeds creamware, however, every edge and corner seems to have been deliberately rounded off, so that it lacks the pleasing sharp and clear-cut appearance of Leeds creamware. Much of Turner's

[1] Plates with somewhat similar prints may be found bearing the impressed marks of such factories as Wedgwood, Herculaneum and Hull.

29A, B FIGURES OF THE SEASONS: A, Spring and Summer; B, Autumn and Winter, pale cream, enamelled in various colours. Figure of Spring marked 'Neale & Co' impressed
NEALE, HANLEY, about 1780, ht. 5½ in (14 cm)
Fitzwilliam Museum, Cambridge. See page 74

creamware was exported to Holland, and Dutch-painted plates bearing the impressed mark 'TURNER' (Appendix III: 121) are not uncommon. Some of these portray the story of 'The Prodigal Son' in enamel painting, while others which were enamelled with a crude but decorative 'Virgin and Child' were sold to pilgrims visiting the shrine at Kevelaar (Plate 30A). Some of Turner's creamware was enamelled at Yarmouth by Absolon whose name is sometimes found painted under pieces of creamware. Absolon was an independent decorator who obtained creamware in the white for enamelling, not only from Turner, but from Davenport and other factories of the late eighteenth and early nineteenth centuries. His painting was very inferior to the best creamware enamelling and usually consisted of landscapes or flowers painted in sepia, sometimes relieved with pale green (Plate 33). As well as some unsuccessful enamelling on creamware figures, one of which is at the British Museum, he is also known to have done transfer-printing in black and gilded decoration on glass. Other enamelling on Turner's creamware was usually over-careful and timid although the execution was good.

Some plates marked 'TURNER' were decorated with transfer-prints engraved by John Aynsley of Lane End (see Appendix III: 126 and respective note).[1] Dessert-services in pearlware with looped borders and underglaze blue 'feathered' edging are sometimes found with the impressed mark 'TURNER' underneath (see Appendix III: 121). He is said to have been one of the first in Staffordshire to print in underglaze blue. In 1780 Turner entered into partnership with Andrew Abbott, a china decorator and agent who had a warehouse at 82 Fleet Street, London and took James Mist into partnership. Abbott died in 1819. Turner died in 1786 and was succeeded by his sons, William and John. The works were closed about 1803.

ELIJAH MAYER OF HANLEY

Elijah Mayer began as an enameller in 1770. A *Directory of Principal Manufacturers and Merchants in the Counties of Stafford, Chester and Lancaster* for 1787 has the following entry: 'Handley—Elijah Mayer, enameller.' This entry suggests that in 1787 he was an enameller only. Chaffers in *Marks and Monograms* gives the impressed mark 'E. MAYER. 1784'; so that there is no doubt that he was actually potting in 1784. It is probable that he had been making creamware on a small scale for a number of years previous to this, as well as doing his enamelling for which he was better known at that time. This consisted for the main part of copies of Wedgwood's creamware border patterns. The creamware made by Mayer is of good quality, very light in weight, with a glaze of apple-green tint which distinguishes it from most other makes of creamware. Tea-services were frequently fluted, with vertical blue

[1] A well-known engraving by John Aynsley entitled 'Keep within compass' is illustrated in the *Schreiber Collection Catalogue* (Victoria and Albert Museum), Vol. II, Plate 59, No. 411.

30A PLATE, pale cream, enamelled in Holland with 'Our Lady of Kevelaar' in red,
maroon, green and yellow. Mark 'TURNER' impressed
LANE END, about 1780, diam. 10 in (20.5 cm)
Zeitlin Collection. See page 76

30B MONTEITH, pale cream, uncoloured. Impressed mark 'TURNER'
LANE END, about 1780, length 17 in (43.2 cm)
Victoria and Albert Museum

enamelled stripes. Teapots were often straight-sided with curved tops and had a simple ball knob on the cover. His name impressed is also sometimes seen on pierced open-work baskets for cakes or fruit; on creamware with an enamelled brown edge and on plates with religious subjects enamelled in Holland. The Hanley and Shelton directory for the year 1818 has the following entry, 'Elijah Mayer & Son, High Street', showing that at that date Mayer's son Joseph had a share in the business. The works were finally closed in 1830. The marks of Elijah Mayer are illustrated in Appendix III: 117 and 118.

THE WOOD FAMILY OF BURSLEM

This family played a very important part in the history and production of creamware in Staffordshire. There were two main branches of the family which descended from the brothers Ralph and Aaron Wood, sons of Ralph Wood (1677–1753), a miller of Burslem. Ralph Wood (1716–72) and his son Ralph Wood (1748–95) were the makers of the well-known figures decorated with soft underglaze patches of colour. Figures made by the elder Ralph Wood were usually greyish in colour and, unlike the Leeds figures which are glazed throughout, those by the elder Ralph Wood are only glazed on the outside and the hollow interior shows the greyish unglazed body (Colour Plate C). These were sometimes marked with four trees in relief, being a rebus for Wood, or with the impressed mark 'R. WOOD' (Appendix III: 110 and 112). The later figures of this factory which were probably made by the younger Ralph Wood, on the other hand, have a true cream-coloured body (Plate 31); but this also has a greyish appearance sometimes, on account of the glaze which is a greyish-blue with a tendency to green. These later figures are not open throughout but have a closed base and sometimes bear the impressed mark 'RA. WOOD BURSLEM' (Appendix III: 111). Perhaps the best known of the figures made by Ralph Wood the elder and repeated by his son is the 'Vicar and Moses' group. Besides figures and Toby jugs some marked flower-vases occur. In addition to creamware, the Woods also made saltglaze tableware, marked and dated moulds for which are at the Victoria and Albert Museum and British Museum.[1] Brother to the elder Ralph Wood was Aaron Wood (1718–85) the celebrated block-cutter who worked first for Dr. Thomas Wedgwood and from 1746 till 1750 for Thomas Whieldon. Aaron had two sons, William (1746–1808) and Enoch (1759–1840). William was apprenticed to Josiah Wedgwood in 1762 and continued with the firm of Wedgwood all his life, working first at Burslem and later at Etruria. Much of Josiah Wedgwood's Queen's ware is said to have been moulded by him. Enoch was apprenticed to Palmer of Hanley and for a time was a partner with his cousin Ralph. In 1783

[1] A block-mould of a saltglaze cream-jug at the Victoria and Albert Museum is marked 'R.W. 1749'. This mould is illustrated in Bernard Rackham, *Early Staffordshire Pottery*, London, 1951, on Plate 41B.

31   BUST OF NEPTUNE, enamelled in polychrome colours. Impressed mark
'Ra. Wood'
RALPH WOOD THE YOUNGER, BURSLEM, about 1775, ht. $11\frac{7}{8}$ in (30.2 cm)
Victoria and Albert Museum. See page 78

he commenced as master potter at Fountain Place, Burslem, where he was joined by James Caldwell in 1790, and the firm became Wood and Caldwell. In 1819 he bought Caldwell out, and the firm took the name Enoch Wood and Sons until about 1846, when it was closed. Enoch Wood was a creamware potter and is best known for his figures, which are usually painted in enamel colours. His busts of Wesley, Voltaire and others are familiar, and some figures bearing the Wedgwood mark would seem to have been made by him to Wedgwood's order (see page 72 and Appendix III:50). In addition to figures, however, Enoch Wood made creamware for the table. Twig-baskets for fruit sometimes bear the mark 'ENOCH WOOD' impressed (Appendix III:115), and the mark 'w (∗∗∗)' (Appendix III:113), which is believed to be his mark, is sometimes to be found on pieces from creamware dessert-services, such as the large covered cream-bowl illustrated (Plate 32) and another at the Fitzwilliam Museum, Cambridge. The cover of these bowls has the type of flower knob which is illustrated in Appendix I, Plate VII, fig. 7. In addition to creamware, Enoch Wood produced many other types of ware such as jasper, basaltes, and porcelain.

SHORTHOSE AND HEATH OF HANLEY

This factory made a good quality creamware at the end of the eighteenth century though the glaze sometimes shows considerable crazing. Cake-baskets with pierced open-work sides and twig-baskets with the name 'SHORTHOSE' impressed are not uncommon (Appendix III:127 and 128). These were sometimes coated with a yellow glaze. Dessert-ware was sometimes decorated with transfer-printed designs in red, to which enamelled borders in bright turquoise blue were occasionally added. Shorthose creamware is sometimes found painted by Absolon of Yarmouth, who bought it in the white. Some transfer-printed ware coloured over in enamels is impressed with the Shorthose mark.

WILLIAM ADAMS OF TUNSTALL

A number of potters of the name William Adams, who were descended from William Adams, master potter of Burslem (died 1617), were renowned for printing on creamware in underglaze-blue towards the end of the eighteenth century. Of these William Adams of Greengates, Tunstall, who was born in 1745, and worked from 1777–1805, made a fine quality creamware which he painted in underglaze-blue. This was very soon superseded however by printing in underglaze-blue on pearlware. His name is sometimes found impressed on the ware (Appendix III:119 and 120). For further information on this family of potters, see W. Turner, *William Adams an Old English Potter* (London, 1904).

32 COVERED CREAM-BOWL, pale cream, enamelled in blue, green and red.
Impressed mark 'W (∗∗∗)'
ENOCH WOOD, about 1790, ht. 10¾ in (27.3 cm)
Towner Collection. See page 80

JOHN DAVENPORT OF LONGPORT

John Davenport was born in 1765, and worked from 1794 to 1834. He made a good quality whitish creamware frequently painted with landscapes or flowers in a pale bluish-green colour and sepia by Absolon of Yarmouth (see page 76) (Plate 33). A pale green colour usually formed an edging to creamware plates. About 1820 Davenport produced a deep yellow ware and an orange-buff-coloured ware decorated with landscapes painted in black or red. Blue-printed ware and a fine quality porcelain were also produced by this factory in the nineteenth century. The factory mark was the name 'DAVENPORT' and an anchor, impressed (see Appendix III: 124 and 125). The factory was not finally closed till 1887.

JOSIAH SPODE OF STOKE-ON-TRENT

Josiah Spode was born in 1733. In 1749 he was hired by Thomas Whieldon, and later set up on his own account at Stoke. Spode made a good quality creamware much of which was enamelled with border patterns. These, though often more elaborate, were in much the same style as those found on Wedgwood's creamware.

From 1783 until his death in 1797, Spode's chief manufacture was pearlware printed in underglaze-blue. During this period Copeland became a partner with Spode and the firm became Spode and Copeland. After Josiah Spode's death, his son Josiah continued the manufacture of underglaze-blue printing, and in 1800 commenced making porcelain. Josiah Spode the second died in 1827 and shortly afterwards the firm traded under the name Copeland and Garrett. The mark used on the creamware of this factory was the name 'SPODE' impressed (Appendix III: 122 and 123).

JOHN AND GEORGE ROGERS OF DALE HALL, BURSLEM

This factory was founded about 1780. Besides blue-printed ware, they produced some fine whiteware, decorated with flowers beautifully painted in enamel colours.[1] The name 'ROGERS' is sometimes found impressed on the ware.

---

[1] See *Schreiber Collection Catalogue* (Victoria and Albert Museum), Vol. II, Plate 53, No. 429.

33   DISH, pale cream, painted with flowers in black and pale bluish-green by
ABSOLON and edged with pale bluish-green enamel. Marks 'DAVENPORT' over
an anchor impressed and 'Absolon Yarm No. 25' painted in black
DAVENPORT, about 1800, length 8 in (20.3 cm)
Victoria and Albert Museum. See pages 76 and 82

LAKIN AND POOLE OF BURSLEM

This factory produced some fine quality creamware of a very pale colour towards the end of the eighteenth century. It was sometimes painted with exotic birds in brightly coloured enamels. This pottery also produced an attractive drab-coloured ware enamelled with flowers in black, sepia and white. Figures decorated in enamel colours, blue-printed ware and lustre ware were among the other productions of this factory. The usual mark was the name 'LAKIN' impressed.

THOMAS AND HERBERT MINTON OF STOKE

Thomas Minton formed his works in 1793 but actual production did not take place till 1796. Most of the wares then produced were printed in underglaze-blue. The firm then traded under the name Thomas Minton and Sons. Among the great variety of wares made by the Minton factory, mention must be made of some undecorated creamware which in form and colour resembled that of the eighteenth century, but which possessed a different composition of body and glaze. This was made by Herbert Minton, about 1840. Such pieces are sometimes impressed with the mark 'H.M. & CO.'.

JOHN HEATH OF BURSLEM

The impressed marks of this potter are 'HEATH' or 'J.H.'. These are frequently found under plates which are either enamel painted, underglaze-blue painted on pearlware or enamel painted in Holland with scenes from the story of 'The Prodigal Son'.

WILLIAM BACCHUS OF LITTLE FENTON

Excavations recently carried out on the site of Whieldon's works at Little Fenton (also known as Fenton Vivian) have resulted in the discovery of a large number of creamware shards nearby. Some of these bear the impressed mark of 'WB' in monogram. It is thought that this was the mark of William Bacchus. The shards include portions of plates with moulded borders of shell, diamond, feather or silver patterns; teapot spouts of the shell pattern and double handles with terminals (Appendix I, Plate X: 11, 11A).

34A PAIR OF CANDLESTICKS, pale cream WHITEHEAD, HANLEY, about 1800, ht. 10½ in (26.2 cm). Illustrated Whitehead catalogue, No. 105
Towner Collection. See page 89

34B CRUET with three bottles and one castor (originally two castors), with inscriptions in German painted in black; pale cream, the handle made of wood WHITEHEAD, HANLEY, about 1800, ht. 9¾ in (24.3 cm). Illustrated Whitehead catalogue, No. 73
Walford Collection. See page 89

JAMES AND CHARLES WHITEHEAD OF HANLEY

Christopher Whitehead is listed in a directory of 1784 as a potter of Shelton. Nothing is known of his productions. He was succeeded about 1793 by his two sons James and Charles Whitehead who were bankrupt soon after 1810. The Whiteheads are principally known by a pattern book which they published in 1798. They were then working in Hanley. The designs in this book show a close affinity with those in the Wedgwood, Leeds and Castleford pattern books from which many of the engravings were clearly derived. Not many pieces of

35A   TEAPOT, pale cream, transfer-printed in black from an engraving by WILLIAM GREATBATCH and enamelled over in red, green, yellow and rosy purple. 'Captain Cook being directed by Britannia', inscribed 'W.R.' (or 'W.R.O.') 'No. 129'.
GREATBATCH, about 1780, ht. 5¾ in (14.5 cm)
Formerly Towner Collection. See pages 38 and 40

35B   TEAPOT, pale cream, transfer-printed in black from an engraving by WILLIAM GREATBATCH, and enamelled over in red, green, purple and yellow, and inscribed 'The Hon'ble Aug'tus Keppel'
GREATBATCH, about 1780, ht. 5¼ in (13.3 cm)
Formerly Towner Collection. See pages 38 and 40

36A TEAPOT, pale cream, transfer-printed in black from an engraving by WILLIAM
GREATBATCH, and enamelled over in red, green, yellow and rosy purple.
Inscribed 'The Prodigal Son in Excess'; on the reverse 'The Prodigal Son in
Misery'
GREATBATCH, about 1780, ht. 4¾ in (12 cm)
Shand Kydd Collection. See pages 38, 40 and 150

36B TEAPOT, pale cream, transfer-printed in black from an engraving by WILLIAM
GREATBATCH, and enamelled over in red, green, yellow and rosy purple.
Inscribed 'The XII Houses of Heaven' and 'Published as the Act directs Jany 4
1778 by W. Greatbatch Lane Delf Staffordshire'; on the reverse 'The Fortune
Teller'
GREATBATCH, about 1780, ht. 5 in (12.7 cm)
Formerly Gollancz Collection. See pages 38 and 40

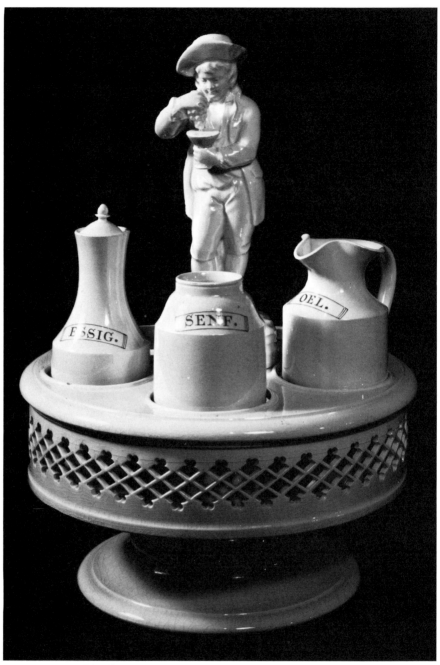

37   CRUET with three bottles, with inscriptions in German painted in red; pale cream. Impressed mark 'P & F. WARBURTON'
COBRIDGE, about 1790, ht. 11⅛ in (28.3 cm)
Leeds Art Galleries. See pages 32 and 89

creamware of their manufacture have so far been identified. The cruet and candlesticks illustrated (Plate 34A and B) can however be attributed to them with some certainty as they correspond exactly with the illustrations in the Whitehead pattern book even to the wooden handle on the cruet. The candlesticks are illustrated on Plate 22, No. 105, and the cruet on Plate 13, No. 73 of the Whitehead pattern book where it is described as a 'Round Waiter, Complete'. As far as is known the wares of this factory are unmarked. The Whitehead creamware seems to be fairly distinctive being very pale in colour with an unusually hard glaze.

PETER AND FRANCIS WARBURTON OF COBRIDGE

Peter and Francis Warburton were makers of a fine quality creamware at Cobridge during the last quarter of the eighteenth century. A cruet of their manufacture is illustrated on Plate 37 and bears the mark 'P & F. WARBURTON' impressed (Appendix III: 130). Some creamware with the mark 'WARBUR-TON' impressed (Appendix III: 129) is probably also of their manufacture. In 1802 after the dissolution of the partnership, Francis established a pottery in France at La Charité-Sur-Loire (see pages 184 and 186).

Note: Examples of the later ware of William Greatbatch are shown on Plates 35 and 36. The attribution is confirmed by the recent discovery (1977) of the Greatbatch site. For a fuller account of this and the earlier Greatbatch wares see pages 34–42.

Chapter 5

COCKPIT HILL, DERBY

From an agreement of 5 October 1767 we learn the names of the original partners of this pottery, namely, William Butts, John Heath, Thomas Rivett and Ralph Steane, and that the deed of partnership was dated 25 December 1753, but that the partnership itself was reckoned as from 11 November 1751. How long the factory had been working before this we do not know but it seems likely that it was founded in 1750. The factory buildings formed a square on Cockpit Hill which still bears that name. The principal building, called New House, was added in 1760 and existed till within fairly recent years.

John Heath, who was largely instrumental in forming the Derby China factory, and his brother Christopher, who later became a partner of the Cockpit Hill works, were bankers. John became mayor of Derby. Rivett owned the land on which the works were built and Butts was responsible for the working of the pottery. The works were closed in 1779 due to the failure of the banks, when the two Heath brothers became bankrupt.

The *Derby Mercury* states, 'On 29 February 1780 a sale of auction took place of a large quantity of Earthen and China Ware at the pot works on Cockpit Hill in Derby being the stock-in-trade of Messrs. John and Christopher Heath, bankrupts.' The advertisements for subsequent sales appeared in the *Derby Mercury* of 17, 24 and 31 March and again on 7 April 1780. These read:

> To the Merchants, Traders and Dealers in Earthenware. To be sold without reserve (and considerably under the usual Wholesale Price). At the Derby Pot Manufactury, A large quantity of Earthenware, being the whole stock in trade of that great and extensive factory commonly known by the name of Derby Pot Works, consisting of an assortment of enamell'd and blue and white useful China: a large quantity of Enamelled Cream Ware, and plain Cream tentable ware; a great quantity of White stone and Brown Ware. N.B. The aforesaid Earthenware etc. will be opened for sale on the 4th and 6th of April and continue selling every Tuesday and Thursday until the whole is dispos'd off on which days (but no others in the week) a proper person will attend the Sale.

38A TEAPOT, deep cream, transfer-printed in black from an engraving by THOMAS
RADFORD. Mark 'Pot Works in Derby' in the print. On the reverse the 'Tea
Party' marked 'Radford Sc. Derby Pot Works' in the print
COCKPIT HILL, DERBY, about 1765, ht. 4 in (10.1 cm)
British Museum. See page 92

38B TEAPOT, deep cream transfer-printed in black, signed with an anchor and the
word 'Derby' in the print. On the reverse the print 'L'Amour'
COCKPIT HILL, DERBY, about 1765, ht. 4½ in (11.5 cm)
Fitzwilliam Museum, Cambridge. See page 92

This Earthenware will be sold in different lots and is well worth the notice of Pot Carriers in and about the neighbourhood of Coleorton Moor.

No less a quantity than two horse loads will be sold to one person.

From this advertisement it is evident that the Derby Pot Works produced plain and enamelled creamware amongst other products which included 'white stone', i.e. saltglaze, and brownware, which was probably similar to the Nottingham salt-glazed stoneware.

The word 'tentable' in the advertisement is undoubtedly a printer's error for 'teatable'.

An 'assortment of Blue and White China' probably refers to porcelain and porcelainous wares which were made at the factory at one time. Creamware and saltglaze however are specified as being in 'large' and 'great' quantities respectively, and were no doubt the chief products of the factory.

Transfer-Printing

In 1764 John Heath and William Duesbury acquired the process of printing from Richard Holdship, and it is through the marked transfer-printed ware that we have become acquainted with the Cockpit Hill creamware generally. That the marks are printed and not incised or impressed is of course unsatisfactory, but all the marked pots are so consistent in character, design, potting and glazing that there is no doubt whatever that they are all of one manufacture, and it is hardly conceivable that they could have been made by any other factory than Cockpit Hill, especially as some of them bear the words 'Pot Works in Derby'.

The following marked pieces are now known:

1. Teapot in the British Museum (Plate 38A), height 4 inches; globular; faceted spout; ribbed loop handle (the ribs are barely visible owing to bad moulding); knob, flat and round on a very short stem, like a button, pierced through the centre to form a steam-hole. The pot has a very slight outward turn at the base, suggesting a diminutive foot-rim. The glaze is a dirty yellow, badly crazed all over. A noticeable feature of the crazing is a tendency for it to run in strong horizontal lines. The vertical cracks are generally less marked. Though the glaze is brilliant, the general appearance is somewhat dirty, and it is probable that originally the glaze was a bright greenish-yellow which has become stained in use. On one side is a version of the 'Tea Party', transfer-printed in black, and marked in the print 'Radford Sc. Derby Pot Works'. On the reverse is a print of the 'Push-cart' signed 'Pot Works in Derby'. On the cover is a print of three cherubs within a husk border (Appendix III: 4 and 5).

2. An almost identical teapot was formerly in the author's collection.

3. Teapot in the Glaisher Collection at the Fitzwilliam Museum, Cambridge (Plate 38B), height 4½ inches; globular with the greatest width slightly above the centre; faceted spout showing traces of a small moulded pattern (Appendix I, Plate I: 2); scroll handle (Appendix I, Plate IV: 3B);

39A   TEAPOT, deep cream, enamelled in red monochrome
      COCKPIT HILL, DERBY, about 1765, ht. 4 in (10.1 cm)
      Towner Collection. See page 97

39B   TEAPOT, deep cream, enamelled in red, black and green, flowers on the reverse
      COCKPIT HILL, DERBY, about 1770, ht. 4 in (10.1 cm)
      Towner Collection. See page 96

knob, a pierced formalized upright flower. The glaze is a brilliant greenish-yellow, crazed in strong horizontal lines and is speckled with sanding. The underside is unglazed and has a circular concavity in the centre about 1 inch in diameter and ⅛ inch in depth. Transfer-printed in black, on one side 'L'Amour', on the reverse a combination of 'Tea Party' and 'Push-cart'. Marked in the print with an anchor and 'Derby' (Appendix III: 6).[1]

4. Jug in the Derby Museum,[2] height 4 inches; flat loop handle with pinched end. The glaze is a bright greenish-yellow, crazed all over with a strong horizontal tendency, and is very unevenly and badly applied. Transfer-printed in black on one side 'L'Amour'; on the reverse 'The Garden Conversation'; marked in the print with an anchor and the word 'Derby' (Appendix III: 6).

5. Teapot in the Derby Museum and Art Gallery,[3] height 4¼ inches; globular with the greatest width slightly above the centre; faceted spout; ribbed loop handle; pierced button knob; transfer-printed in black, on one side a portrait bust of Catherine II of Russia surrounded by an inscription in Russian, marked in the print 'T. Radford Sc. Derby'. On the reverse the Russian arms with the date 1765 and the words 'Rouble Coin' on either side, the whole surrounded by a floral border. The cover is decorated with two floral sprays.

6. Plate in the Derby Museum, six-lobed 'Royal Pattern'; diameter 8¼ inches; clumsily potted with bright greenish-yellow glaze unevenly applied and badly crazed, the crazing running in long uneven lines; transfer-printed with two lovers seated under a tree watching two dogs at play, under the inscription 'Summer Amusements'. Three groups of flowers round the rim, marked in the print with an anchor and the word 'Derby' (Appendix III: 6).

7. Plate in the Mint Museum, Charlotte, U.S.A.; six-lobed 'Royal Pattern'; diameter 8¼ inches; similar to No. 6, but decorated with a print of 'L'Amour' and the words 'French Amour'. It is marked with an anchor and the word 'Derby' in the print (Appendix III: 6).

8. Teapot in the Willett Collection, Brighton. Transfer-printed in black with a portrait of John Wilkes on one side; signed 'T. Radford' in the print, and 'No. 45' on the reverse.

Other known Cockpit Hill transfer-printed pieces are a teapot at the Fitzwilliam Museum, Cambridge, on which the print is signed by Thomas Rothwell who also engraved for the Cockpit Hill factory at one time, and a teapot in the Zeitlin Collection with a masonic print which though unsigned was clearly engraved by Thomas Radford, showing that he was still engraving for the Cockpit Hill factory well into the 1770s.

---

[1] The anchor is the rebus of Richard Holdship who introduced transfer-printing to Derby in 1764.
[2] Illustrated in Geoffrey Godden, 'Derby Pot Works, Cockpit Hill', in *Transactions of the English Ceramic Circle*, Vol. III, Part IV, London, 1955; on Plate 67A and Plate 68B and C.
[3] Ibid., Plates 65C and D.

40A TEAPOT, deep cream, enamelled in red, black and green
     COCKPIT HILL, DERBY, about 1765, ht. $5\frac{1}{4}$ in (13.3 cm)
     Formerly Towner Collection. See page 96
40B TEAPOT, deep cream, enamelled in red, black and green
     COCKPIT HILL, DERBY, about 1765, ht. $4\frac{7}{8}$ in (12.2 cm)
     Victoria and Albert Museum. See page 96

From the above pieces the characteristics of Cockpit Hill creamware can be enumerated as follows:

1. A brilliant glaze, which is bright greenish-yellow in colour.
2. The glaze is often crazed and sometimes shows evidence of sanding; the crazing has a tendency to run in long lines in places; elsewhere it forms a fairly even mesh.
3. The potting and general workmanship are often rather poor.
4. The spouts are often faceted (Appendix I, Plate 1:3).
5. The knobs are often like a button, and are pierced for the steam-hole (Appendix I, Plate VIII:16).
6. The greatest width of the teapots is usually slightly above the centre.
7. The undersides of pots are usually unglazed and sometimes have a central concavity about 1 inch in diameter. (The undersides are sometimes partially glazed where the glaze has run accidentally.)
8. Scroll handles are nearly always cut off square and not divided into two lobes as in the Wedgwood variety.

Enamelling, Forms and Details

A number of examples of enamelled creamware with the above characteristics are known, though the general quality and workmanship of these is usually superior to those of the transfer-printed pieces.

The creamware teapot with enamelled flower decoration in red, black and green (Plate 40A), corresponds in every respect, except for the decoration, with the marked transfer-printed teapot in the Glaisher Collection already described (Plate 38B). It has a brilliant glaze which is bright greenish-yellow in colour and is badly crazed in long running lines. It is badly sanded, unglazed underneath, and the scroll handle is cut off square at the base and not divided. Underneath are four black strokes and a green spot, which were probably made by the enameller in trying out his colours. Closely allied to this last is a teapot at the Victoria and Albert Museum (Plate 40B) whose chief difference lies in the form of handle. The painting consists of a red rose with cherries, lilies and honeysuckle. We find this same painting repeated again on another early group also possessing other typical Cockpit Hill characteristics of glaze etc. Pieces of this group illustrated here are a caddy (Plate 42A), a teapot with crabstock handle and spout (Plate 42B), and a tankard (Plate 41).

Sometimes one finds Cockpit Hill creamware painted with birds by the Derby porcelain bird painter. The teapot illustrated (Plate 39B) is of better quality generally than the transfer-printed pieces though possessing the usual characteristics of glaze, crazing etc. It has the button knob and scroll handle with a blunt end and is unglazed underneath with a slight cavity in the centre. The long running lines of crazing are very discernible, but we are now introduced to a different form of spout (Appendix I, Plate I:6). The enamelling is in soft Indian red, black and green; on the reverse side is some delicate and charming flower painting.

C FIGURE OF A DUTCH GIRL, decorated with coloured glazes. Mark 'R. WOOD'
impressed
RALPH WOOD senior, about 1770, ht. 6 in (15.2 cm)
Victoria and Albert Museum. See page 78

D COVERED CREAM-BOWL, enamel painted
MELBOURNE, about 1775, ht. $9\frac{1}{2}$ in (23.5 cm)
Walford Collection. See page 110

41   TANKARD, deep cream, enamelled in red, black, green and yellow
      COCKPIT HILL, DERBY, about 1765, ht. 6¾ in (17 cm)
      Towner Collection. See page 96

A teapot of the same form as the marked British Museum teapot (Plate 38A)
and possessing all its dominant features but painted in red monochrome, is
illustrated (Plate 39A).

Similar in form to the last is a teapot in the Castle Museum, Norwich but on
this we find a different style of flower painting which is characterized by a red
rose and smaller daisy-like flowers with short upper petals and longer lower
ones (Plate 43A). A teapot in the Leeds Art Galleries links this last teapot with
later Cockpit Hill ones by having the early button knob and faceted spout but a
double handle with terminals and painting of Chinese figures (Plate 43B). It

42A   TEA-CADDY, deep cream,
enamelled in red, black, green
and yellow
COCKPIT HILL, DERBY, about
1765, ht. 4⅝ in (11.3 cm)
Walford Collection. See page 96

42B   TEAPOT, deep cream,
enamelled in red, black, green
and yellow
COCKPIT HILL, DERBY, about
1765, ht. 4½ in (10.1 cm)
*Formerly Towner Collection.
See page 96*

43A TEAPOT, deep cream, enamelled in red, green and black
COCKPIT HILL, DERBY, about 1770, ht. $4\frac{1}{4}$ in (10.8 cm)
Castle Museum, Norwich. See page 97
43B TEAPOT, deep cream, enamelled in red, green, purple, yellow and black
COCKPIT HILL, DERBY, about 1770, ht. 5 in (13 cm)
Leeds Art Galleries. See page 97

44A   TEAPOT, deep cream, enamelled in red, black, green, purple and yellow
COCKPIT HILL, DERBY, about 1770, ht. 6 in (15.2 cm)
Towner Collection. See page 102
44B   Reverse side of 44A

45A SCREW-TOP BOX, deep cream, enamelled in red, black, green, purple and yellow
COCKPIT HILL, DERBY, about 1770, diam. 3 in (7.5 cm)
Towner Collection. See page 102

45B TEAPOT, deep cream, enamelled in red, black, green, purple and yellow
COCKPIT HILL, DERBY, about 1775, ht. 5¾ in (14.6 cm)
Towner Collection. See page 102

presents us too with a new teapot form which was globular with a concave shoulder. Teapots of this form which probably date from about 1770 are usually painted with flowers which include purple daisies on one side and Chinese figures or sometimes birds, on the other (Plates 44A and B). Cherries, too, remained a favourite subject. The Chinese figures are by the same painter who decorated both some Derby porcelain and Melbourne creamware. The same flower painting occurs on a Cockpit Hill screw-top box (Plate 45A) which has on its top some delightful painting of a young man wearing a purple jacket, seated in a landscape. Another screw-top box (Colour Plate H) is painted with a bird by the Derby bird painter. The cover of Cockpit Hill teapots at this time was surmounted by a convolvulus flower knob which on enamelled ware invariably had a red rim. The double handle was without any ribbing but was finished by terminals usually consisting of a flower and two leaves, but there were a number of other patterns (Appendix I, Plate VI:8). The spout, too, was changed to a plain one with a slight suggestion of leaves at its base (Appendix I, Plate III:5).

Just before the closure of the pottery a 'square'-shaped teapot was introduced (Plate 45B). This was straight-sided with an indented loop handle; otherwise the characteristics are the same as before.

One of the enamellers at the Cockpit Hill factory is known to have been Mundy Simpson. He had formerly been an apprentice there and later became a flower painter and removed to the Derby China works.

Colour-glazed Ware

Tortoiseshell and colour-glazed ware generally were made at Cockpit Hill in quantity. This was often of very fine quality and possessed the same characteristics as the enamelled and transfer-printed wares; otherwise the technique of applying the glazes is very similar to Whieldon's.

The pineapple pattern was produced at Cockpit Hill in saltglaze, colour-glazed ware and both enamelled and plain creamware. The teapot illustrated (Plate 46A) not only has typical characteristics of glaze, indented base etc. but also a seal mark (Appendix III:193) consisting of the disguised letters 'ChD' (Cockpit Hill Derby). The colour-glazed teapot illustrated (Plate 46B) has the typical Derby glaze and handle and a strawberry pattern spout (Appendix I, Plate III:3) which also occurs on Cockpit Hill enamelled creamware and saltglaze but is not known on the wares of any other factory. The Cockpit Hill factory undoubtedly produced quantities of plain undecorated creamware, but very little of this has come to light, presumably it was not thought worthwhile to take care of it. A fine example is in the Greg Collection, Manchester City Art Gallery.

From the known examples of Cockpit Hill pottery it becomes apparent that this factory had a very large output and must have been one of the largest earthenware factories in the country at that time. Drawings of some of the moulded details believed to be peculiar to the Cockpit Hill pottery will be

46A TEAPOT, deep cream. Impressed seal mark, Appendix III, No. 193
     COCKPIT HILL, DERBY, about 1765, ht. 5½ in (14 cm)
     Towner Collection. See page 102
46B TEAPOT, deep cream, coated with coloured glazes of green, slate–blue, yellow
     and manganese
     COCKPIT HILL, DERBY, about 1765, ht. 5 in (12.7 cm)
     Villiers Collection. See page 102

found in Appendix I. It should be noted that in the eighteenth century both styles—'Cockpit Hill Derby' and 'Derby Pot Works'—were used.

The following extract is from *The Old Derby China Factory* by John Haslem, 1876:

> At that time (1780) there was a large stock of earthenware at the Cockpit Hill Works, some of which was disposed of by auction and in other ways in the town. Duesbury became possessed of a large portion of this stock, which he took to Ireland, and disposed of in Dublin advantageously. The remnant of the Cockpit Hill stock was removed to the China works on the Nottingham road and remained there in the old part of the factory until nearly 1830 when it was sold in a lump to a dealer in the town, a circumstance which the writer well remembers. . . . A much larger factory was erected early in the present century [nineteenth] on the eastern side of the old one. . . . these new works were erected for the purpose of manufacturing creamware and earthenware and both were made for a short period. The creamware, judging by the few known specimens extant was scarcely inferior either in the fine quality of the paste or in design and execution, to Wedgwood's creamware.

In actual fact, creamware was made at this new pottery for little more than a year, between July 1798 and November 1799.

Chapter 6

MELBOURNE POTTERY, DERBYSHIRE

During recent years the discovery of a large quantity of creamware shards near Melbourne, a small Derbyshire town close to the Leicestershire border, has established that the wares produced there were of a very superior quality and the pottery one of considerable importance though probably not large. After its closure, seemingly in the early years of the nineteenth century, a farm was built on the site known as Furnace Farm. Here the remains of kilns, kiln furniture and the shards were found. Soon after the excavations were made the area was flooded to form a reservoir so that no further excavations now seem possible. The site lies one mile south of Melbourne and about eight miles south of Derby.

The sole piece of documentary evidence so far known to us is an advertisement in the *Derby Mercury* of 8 March 1776 which reads:

> Wanted a journeyman potter at Melbourne, Derbyshire that can throw and turn cream-coloured ware. A sober man may have constant employ and good wages.

It is to be hoped however that further newspaper notices relating to the pottery will be discovered in due course. The rent books of the Melbourne Hall estate upon which Furnace Farm was situated may also be another possible source of documentation although examination of these has so far been without result.

Our knowledge of the wares produced by the Melbourne Pottery has been entirely formed therefore from the shards found on the site. These have also provided us with approximate dates for the duration of the factory and a few other facts relative to the history of the pottery. They were found to be lying in layers where they had fallen over a period of years and not mixed together as they would have been if brought from somewhere else and tipped there. The lowest layer sloped from a few inches under the surface to a depth of approximately four feet and consisted of creamware, a few pieces of white saltglaze and lumps of white clay and ash. Above the creamware was a layer of brown saltglaze of the Nottingham type and above this a layer of coarse utilitarian ware, made about the end of the eighteenth century. Finally, heaped on top of these were masses of kiln furniture—saggers, stilts and all the debris of a sometime pottery. There is no doubt therefore that this was the actual site of the pottery. The three layers, each consisting of a different class of ware, may well represent different ownerships under which the pottery came, with a possible interval of time between them. In this chapter we shall only be concerned with the earliest period or ownership when creamware and saltglaze were being manufactured.

Although the vast majority of shards were in the biscuit, there was a sprinkling of glazed ones, the varying colour of which ranged from a very deep shade of cream to the very palest milk-white. It can be accepted as a principle that the tonal range of creamware is a direct indication of its age—the deeper the tone, the earlier it is and conversely, the paler the tone, the more recent its date of manufacture. Hence it is that we can say that the deepest creamware shards found at Melbourne were made during the 1760s and the palest about 1780. Thus the life of the factory seems to have roughly coincided with the creamware output of the Cockpit Hill factory only a few miles away. There may be some significance in this although the wares produced by the two factories are for the most part so different. At least one enameller however, as we shall see later, decorated some of the wares of both these factories as well as some of the Derby porcelain factory.

The Shards
A considerable variety of shards was found, although the area uncovered was not more than twenty feet square, which must have been only a very small fraction of the whole pottery area. Some of the shards show a singularity of design which is extremely helpful in the task of discovering the ware made by the Melbourne Pottery. Instances of this are the handle with a sharp spine running up the back (Appendix I, Plate VI:6); the spout with the rounded lobes at the base (Appendix I, Plate III:6); flower knobs pierced through the flower to form a steam-vent (Appendix I, Plate VIII:4 and 12); and the plate border, that for reference sake I have styled the 'cock's-tail' border (Appendix I, Plate XI:4). Less obvious, though nevertheless equally determinate, are the forms of handle terminal and especially the reeding of the handle itself (Appendix I, Plate X:4 and 7) which at first sight would appear to be like those made at Leeds, but which will be found to differ from them on closer inspection, or indeed from those of other factories. This will be apparent if the versions produced at the two factories in question are compared: Appendix I, Plate X:7 and Appendix I, Plate IX:2, the latter being the Leeds example. Another factory difference which is only apparent on close inspection is the 'feather' border. The various factory types of this border will be found in Appendix I, Plate XI, where the differences can be noted. The Melbourne version comprises eight barbs. Six of these are equally spaced but the seventh is very diminutive and is merged into the eighth which is unusually large

47A PLATE, medium cream, enamelled in purple monochrome. Diamond-beaded
border, Appendix I, Plate XI:5. Two nicks in foot-ring
MELBOURNE, about 1768, width 9¼ in (23.5 cm)
Towner Collection. See page 118

47B PLATE, deep cream, enamelled in thick green monochrome. Feather border,
Appendix I, Plate XI:8. Two nicks in foot-ring
MELBOURNE, about 1765, diam. 9¾ in (24.7 cm)
Towner Collection. See page 118

48   TAPER-STICK, deep cream, enamelled in purple monochrome
MELBOURNE, about 1765, ht. 6¾ in (17.2 cm)
Towner Collection. See page 110

49A CAKE-DISH, medium cream. Diamond-beaded border, Appendix I, Plate XI:5.
Terminals, Appendix I, Plate X:12
MELBOURNE, about 1770, length $12\frac{1}{2}$ in (32 cm)
Towner Collection. See page 110

49B CAKE-DISH, medium cream, enamelled in purple monochrome. Diamond-beaded border, Appendix I, Plate XI:5
MELBOURNE, about 1770, length $13\frac{3}{4}$ in (35 cm)
Victoria and Albert Museum. See page 110

(Appendix I, Plate XI:8).[1] On small plates however there are only seven barbs which follows the Wedgwood pattern closely. A type of border pattern found in great profusion among the shards was the 'diamond-beaded' border[2] (Appendix I, Plate XI:5). This was found not only on shards of plates but on various other objects, especially sauceboats. So profuse were they that one might be tempted to suspect any piece found with it to be Melbourne. It was made by a number of other factories[3] however, in most cases with factory variations. Another border found in profusion was the 'reeded' border of silver type (Appendix I, Plate XI:6). This was found in varying widths. There were two varieties found of the ear-shaped handle—a rounded and a flattened section (Appendix I, Plate IV:6)—but both this, the simple loop handle and the straight spout were used by other factories as well. A goat's-head shard was undoubtedly used for a classical vase, but differs from the Cockpit Hill version.

Some Melbourne Characteristics

Some of the small moulded details which appear on the shards have already been mentioned. When two or more of these occur in conjunction with one another we have strong evidence of a Melbourne source, especially when such details are not known on the wares of other factories. Such evidence can be seen on the coffee-pot (Plate 52) and the two teapots at the Castle Museum Norwich (Plate 53A and B) which not only possess the identical Melbourne handle terminal (with additions) but also six rows of diamond beading which was used so much by the pottery. Further the church painted on one of them bears a strong likeness to Melbourne Church which has a large and peculiar weathercock, added in the seventeenth century, very like the one on the teapot, whilst a further characteristic is the convolvulus knob with the three triangular leaves at the base which seems to have been peculiar to the Melbourne Pottery (Appendix I, Plate VII:6). With so much evidence these pieces may well be used as a basis for the attribution of others and lead to later examples in a paler colour. The teapot illustrated on Plate 55A and B, not only possesses the same flower knob with three leaves (Appendix I, Plate VII:6), but has the same spout as that on Plate 53B (Appendix I, Plate III:4).

Much of the ware was pierced and a Melbourne characteristic of this work is the unusually small punchings very often grouped to form a shape somewhat resembling a crown (Colour Plate D). Plates, dishes[4], tureens etc. are often divided into twelve lobes or sides with pierced patterns on alternate lobes.

Characteristic enamelling on the earlier ware is in green or purple monochrome or in red and black in the style of Robinson and Rhodes of Leeds. Later pieces include Chinese figures almost certainly by the same enameller that painted some Cockpit Hill earthenware and Derby porcelain. The green and purple monochrome was often applied thickly, the purple ranging from deep purple to almost a light grey[5]; the green was usually rich and lustrous.

[1]Plate 47B. [2]Plate 47A. [3]Plates 49A, B, 50A. [4]Plate 50B. [5]Plates 48, 50A and 51A.

50A   TEAPOT, medium cream, enamelled in purple monochrome. Diamond-beaded
         border and terminals as on Plate 49A
         MELBOURNE, about 1770, ht. $5\frac{7}{8}$ in (13.8 cm)
         Leeds Art Galleries. See page 110
50B   PLATE, deep cream, pierced and gilded decoration
         MELBOURNE, about 1765, diam. $9\frac{1}{4}$ in (23.5 cm)
         Formerly Towner Collection. See page 110

51A   TUREEN, in the form of a melon, deep cream, enamelled in purple monochrome.
       Terminals, Appendix I, Plate X:6
       MELBOURNE, about 1765, length 8½ in (21.6 cm)
       Victoria and Albert Museum. See page 110
51B   PUNCH-KETTLE, pale cream, transfer-printed in black and enamelled over in
       green, traces of gilding. Terminals, Appendix I, Plate X:12
       MELBOURNE, about 1775, ht. 9 in (23 cm)
       Formerly Gollancz Collection

52 COFFEE-POT, deep cream. Handle terminals, Appendix I, Plate X:7. Flower knob, Appendix I, Plate VII:6
MELBOURNE, about 1768, ht. 9¼ in (23.5 cm)
Towner Collection. See page 110

53A   TEAPOT, deep cream, painted in black and red enamel. Moulded borders,
Appendix I, Plate XI:5. Flower knob, Appendix I, Plate VII:6. Handle
terminals, Appendix I, Plate X:8. Spout, Appendix I, Plate III:4
MELBOURNE, about 1765, ht. 5 in (12.8 cm)
Castle Museum, Norwich. See page 110

53B   TEAPOT, deep cream, painted in black and red enamel. Moulded borders, flower
knob, handle terminals and spout as on Plate 53A
MELBOURNE, about 1765, ht. 5¾ in (14.6 cm)
Castle Museum, Norwich. See page 110

54A PLATE, medium cream, transfer-printed in black. Moulded border, Appendix I,
Plate XI : 5. Two nicks in the foot-ring
MELBOURNE, about 1770, width $9\frac{1}{4}$ in (23.5 cm)
Towner Collection. See page 118

54B PLATE, deep cream, transfer-printed in black. Feather border, Appendix I,
Plate XI : 8. Two nicks in the foot-ring
MELBOURNE, about 1768, diam. $9\frac{5}{8}$ in (24.5 cm)
Towner Collection. See page 124

55A   TEAPOT, pale cream, enamelled in red, green, blue, yellow and black. Flow
knob, Appendix I, Plate VII:6. Handle terminals, Appendix I, Plate IX:1
Spout, Appendix I, Plate III:4
MELBOURNE, about 1775, ht. 6 in (15.25 cm)
Towner Collection. See page 110
55B   Reverse side of Plate 55A

56A   TEAPOT, pale cream, enamelled in red, green, blue, yellow and black. Spout,
      Appendix I, Plate III:4
      MELBOURNE, about 1775, ht. 6 in (15.25 cm)
      Towner Collection
56B   TEAPOT, pale cream, decorated with stripes of green glaze. Cf. Plate 56A
      MELBOURNE, about 1775, ht. 5½ in (13.9 cm)
      City of Manchester Art Galleries

Transfer-printing appears on Melbourne creamware having either the Melbourne version of the feather border or the diamond beading. Much of it consists of a version of the exotic birds designs which seem to have been so popular everywhere. Melbourne specimens so far found are in either red or black (Plate 54A). Another transfer-printed design found on Melbourne plates is unusual on creamware in general, though occurring on the delft tiles printed by Sadler, namely a Chinese lady and small boy fishing. The plate illustrated (Plate 54B) is of a deep cream and therefore an early one. It is not known where the printing on Melbourne creamware was done. The few examples of printed ware so far found do not resemble the Cockpit Hill printing of Holdship and Radford, otherwise one would suppose this to have been a likely source.

Marks on Melbourne Creamware
For the most part factory marks on creamware are rare so that it is not surprising that no Melbourne factory mark has so far been found. Of considerable interest however is a mark that occurs on a great number of Melbourne plates and is not known on the ware of any other factory. This consists of two or sometimes three smooth little nicks about one eighth of an inch apart, cut into the foot-ring with a tool and glazed over. It would seem likely that these marks were used by Melbourne potters and they have helped considerably in the identification of pieces, such as the plates shown on Plate 47A and B, for instance, which though very different from each other in design can be identified as Melbourne, one being octagonal and having the Melbourne diamond beading, the other being round with the Melbourne variety of feather border. They are further linked together by both possessing the two little nicks in the foot-ring and in addition a splutter of the same green enamel used for the decoration of the one occurs under the other which is enamelled in purple. So these form a sound basis for the build-up of other attributions.

Generally speaking, Melbourne creamware is of fine quality and artistically equal to any. Much of it comprises pieces which form groups previously unidentified or loosely assigned to the Leeds Pottery on the grounds of probability but without any positive evidence. A fuller account of the attributive build-up of Melbourne pieces and further illustrations of them will be found in *E.C.C. Transactions*, Volume 8, Part 1, 1971.

Chapter 7

LEEDS POTTERY

Of a group of potteries which existed in South Yorkshire in the eighteenth century, by far the most important was the Leeds Pottery situated at Hunslet, then a village less than a mile south of Leeds.

In the past authors have repeated a statement that the Leeds Pottery was founded in 1760 by two brothers named Green. The origin of this statement can be traced to a letter from Thomas Wilson of Leeds written in 1854 to Henry de la Bèche, Director of the Museum of Practical Geology, Jermyn Street, in answer to his request for information about the Leeds Pottery to include in the Museum catalogue which he was then preparing. Wilson gleaned the information quoted from William Warburton, son of a proprietor of the Leeds Pottery at that time, but the difficulty Wilson had in extracting this information does not inspire one with confidence, especially as the 'two brothers' turn out to be uncle and nephew. Another personal testimony quoted by Wilson was from Petty, son of a neighbouring pottery owner. This gave the Leeds Pottery an even earlier foundation but this too has been found to be equally untrustworthy.

The *Leeds Mercury* for 28 August 1770 states that a large earthenware factory was then being erected near Leeds. In that same year a tract of land called Rushey Pastures upon which the Leeds Pottery is known to have been built, was sold to Richard Humble, one of the Leeds Pottery partners and agent for the Middleton Colliery nearby. Although building had already commenced the completion of the sale was not effected till November 1770. Further, the first insurance policies to be taken out by the Leeds Pottery are dated 10 January 1771, and these state that some of the buildings, such as partners' houses and cottages for workmen, were still unfinished. It is evident therefore that the large factory known as the Leeds Pottery was built in 1770 and it is just possible that production could have started before the end of the year. The jug illustrated on Plate 60 may be one of the first pieces to be produced by the Leeds Pottery in Jack Lane, Hunslet. The question now arises—was this the beginning of the Leeds Pottery or had it a forerunner? It would seem most probable that use would have been made of the men and materials from a smaller pottery in the district if such existed and became available and there are many indications of a forerunner of this kind which cannot be dismissed easily.

In the first place, in spite of much diligent searching, no deed of establishment or original partnership of the Leeds Pottery has been found. Secondly, a firm of china enamellers called Robinson and Rhodes settled at Leeds in 1760 which points to the presence in the neighbourhood of a good supply of wares for them to enamel and we find their enamelling on a great deal of saltglaze and creamware from 1760 onwards. Presumably much of this would have been produced locally. Mention should also be made of a concern of some sort which existed in 1758 run by a group of partners at least one of whom, Henry Ackroyd, was an early partner of the Leeds Pottery.[1] This was situated by the wharf near the river Aire at the far end of the Middleton Colliery Railway, an ideal position both for taking in coal and exporting wares, but there is no proof that this enterprise was in fact a pottery. Maps show the railway, which at first was horse-drawn, running through the Leeds Pottery to which it paid rent for way-leave. An indication, however, of the existence of a precursor of the Leeds Pottery existing before 1770 lies in the fact that certain pieces of creamware possessing strong Leeds characteristics are found with dates prior to 1770 painted on them. Such pieces are rare, but an example is the 'Stonier' jug at the Victoria and Albert Museum (Plate 86). These pieces may have been produced by one or more small potteries working in the Leeds area which having a style of their own, imparted it to the Leeds Pottery when that came to be built. For instance, Dennison's Pottery at Holbeck, only half a mile away and known to have had an early foundation, may perhaps have been a precursor of the Leeds Pottery. The fact that it was put up for sale in 1769, just before the opening of the large new pottery, lends colour to this idea. A coffee-pot which has recently come into the author's possession is of the early type of creamware with strong Leeds characteristics and is incised underneath with the initials 'J.D.' If these stand for Joseph Dennison, owner of the Holbeck Pottery, as seems most probable, a precursor of the Leeds Pottery is confirmed as existing in the immediate neighbourhood of Leeds itself. The coffee-pot which is illustrated on Plate 62 is enamelled in soft red monochrome with a butterfly within a cartouche of scroll-work and flowers, and on the reverse a man playing the bagpipes with a dog sitting beside him. The terminals and convolvulus flower knob (Appendix I, Plate VII:3) are touched with purple, green and yellow enamel. There is also the possibility of an early connexion with the Swinton Pottery. The matter remains inconclusive but on the face of things it would appear that the Leeds Pottery, as such, was first started in 1770.

Our knowledge, however, of the early creamware and where it was made is still very limited and some of the present-day attributions may have to be re-assessed when we know more about it.

---

[1] A second partner was William Green. Joshua Green had a brother of this name. A Leeds jug in the Harrogate Museum is inscribed 'W. Green, 1772'.

57A   SWEETMEAT-DISH, deep cream. Impressed mark 'LEEDS * POTTERY' (Appendix
       III:7)
       LEEDS, about 1770, length 8 in (20.3 cm)
       Towner Collection. See page 124
57B   SAUCEBOAT, deep cream. Handle terminals, Appendix I, Plate IX:5
       LEEDS, about 1770, length 6⅛ in (15.5 cm)
       Towner Collection. See page 124

The first known mention of the Leeds Pottery partners is contained in an
agreement of 11 November 1775, when 'Joshua Green of Middleton, Gent.
and John Green of Hunslet, Potter, with divers others under the firm of
Humble, Green & Co' agreed to set up a water-wheel at Flint Mills, Thorpe
Arch for grinding flints for the Leeds Pottery. The next mention we have is in
1781 when Richard Humble relinquished his partnership. The *Leeds
Intelligencer* of 20 February 1781 announced that 'Notice is hereby given that
the Partnership in the Leeds Pottery between Richard Humble, William
Hartley, Joshua Green, John Green, Henry Ackroyd, John Barwick, Saville
Green and Samuel Wainwright under the firm Humble, Hartley, Greens &
Co., is amicably dissolved and the said William Hartley, Joshua Green, John

Green, Henry Ackroyd, John Barwick, Saville Green and Samuel Wainwright, will hereafter trade under the firm of Hartley, Greens and Company.' The pottery's trade names were therefore: Humble, Green and Co. in 1775; Humble, Hartley, Greens and Co. before 1781; and thereafter, Hartley, Greens and Co. A great many new partnerships were afterwards added and include: Mary Ackroyd, daughter of Henry Ackroyd; Rev. Edward Parsons, who married one of Henry Ackroyd's daughters; William Hartley, junior; Saville Green, junior; Ebenezer Green; Thomas Wainwright; Samuel Wainwright, junior; George Hanson; Nathaniel Clayton and probably others. The bankruptcy of the pottery appears in the *London Gazette* for 6 June 1820, when Mary Ackroyd and Ebenezer Green were declared bankrupts. Samuel Wainwright junior kept the firm working and in 1825 was able to take the pottery out of Chancery and buy the whole concern. He worked it under the name of Samuel Wainwright and Co. until his death from cholera in 1834. The trustees carried on the business under the name of The Leeds Pottery Company until 1842 when it was bought by Stephen Chappell, at which time it traded under the name Stephen and James Chappell, James being Stephen's brother. In 1847 the pottery again became bankrupt, from which date it was worked by Richard Britton, who with Samuel Warburton bought it in 1850. It then traded under the name of Warburton and Britton. Warburton died in 1863, leaving Britton in sole possession till, in 1872, his two sons Broadbent and Alfred became partners with their father and the pottery traded under Richard Britton and Sons until 1878 when it again became bankrupt; it was finally liquidated in 1881.

In this chapter on the Leeds Pottery, we shall only be considering the pottery and its production of creamware until the first bankruptcy in 1820. The cause of the bankruptcy is uncertain and it may be that the pottery which largely depended on its enormous export trade to the Continent was losing this in the early years of the nineteenth century as more and more Continental factories turned to the production of creamware.

It is true that the Leeds Pottery became famous for its creamware and there is no doubt this was its principal product, but it followed the pattern set by Staffordshire and particularly by Thomas Whieldon, of making a great variety of different types of ware. These included saltglaze; glazed red earthenware with cream-coloured reliefs in the Astbury manner; unglazed red stoneware; colour-glazed ware in the Wedgwood-Whieldon manner; green-glazed ware; tortoiseshell ware and unglazed black stoneware; and recently a teapot of a fine quality porcelain impressed 'LEEDS * POTTERY' has been bought for the Leeds Museums and Art Galleries. All these types of ware were made at the Leeds Pottery in addition to its principal product of creamware. Jewitt states that at one time delftware was made at the Leeds Pottery, but there has been no confirmation of this. In this chapter we shall be dealing with Leeds creamware only, but unless its other productions are borne in mind we shall have but a very lop-sided estimate of the pottery.

58A   TEAPOT, deep cream, enamelled in red and black by the Leeds firm of J.
ROBINSON. Terminals and knob touched with green, blue and yellow enamel,
traces of gilding.
LEEDS, about 1770, ht. 4½ in (11.5 cm)
Towner Collection. See pages 124, 128 and 132

58B   TEAPOT, deep cream, enamelled in red and black by the Leeds firm of J.
ROBINSON. Handle, terminals and knob touched with blue, green, yellow and
black enamel
LEEDS, about 1770, ht. 5⅛ in (13 cm)
Towner Collection. See pages 124 and 132

A considerable difficulty is often encountered in assigning creamware to a particular factory. This is largely owing to the scarcity of factory marks and the great similarity of the wares, particularly the early ones, made by factories some of which are completely unknown to us. To add to our difficulties, outside decorators, such as Robinson and Rhodes of Leeds, enamelled the wares of a number of potteries. Through an acquaintance with the known wares of a factory one can often recognize the features, workmanship and other characteristics which can lead to further attributions with some certainty. For instance, because we have the Leeds Pottery pattern and drawing books as well as some marked pieces to guide us, we become acquainted with certain Leeds traits. These include shape, colour, glaze, surface texture, moulded features and decoration. But perhaps the most reliable basis for attribution lies in the moulded details modelled at the factory which usually differ in some degree from those modelled by other factories. This is further explained on page 189 and drawings of these details will be found in Appendix I.

The early Leeds creamware, that is to say the ware made before approximately 1775, was a deep cream colour with a yellowish glaze. The workmanship was of a very high order, proportions were nicely poised and the ware possessed a freedom of technique and invention often lacking in later wares or those of other factories. At first, shapes were similar to saltglaze ones and some of the details correspond with those in general use at that time, such as strap handles for jugs and crabstock ones for teapots. The double handle with terminals was in use before 1770 as may be evidenced by dated pieces such as the 'Stonier' jug (Plate 86) at the Victoria and Albert Museum which is dated 1769. This has strong Leeds features but is evidently from a nearby pottery. At Leeds the double handle was first of all twisted like a rope. Later it became flat and evenly reeded. Both forms were made before 1775. The early terminals were various but were often of a strawberry pattern (Appendix I, Plate IX:2) which, with slight differences, was also used elsewhere, notably at Melbourne. The flower knob at this time was usually a convolvulus with the strawberry or other terminal. Spouts were of types shown in Appendix I. The change in colour from deep to pale cream seems to have occurred rather later at Leeds than at most other factories and though there was a gradual transition over a few years the complete change did not occur till about 1775 or 1776. During this transition period and even before, new moulded details were introduced which link with the later creamware.

Factory marks on the early deep cream-coloured ware are exceedingly rare but one such—a shell sweetmeat-dish (Plate 57A) has the words 'LEEDS * POTTERY' impressed (Appendix III:7). This gives a strong indication of the particular qualities of the ware at that time, such as an uneven colouring and slight crazing. These characteristics match certain other pieces exactly such as the sauceboat and teapots illustrated (Plates 57B and 58A and B). From the last we become aware of the type of enamelling used on much of the early Leeds creamware, a great deal of which was done by the firm of Robinson and

59A TEAPOT, deep cream, enamelled in red and black by the Leeds firm of J. ROBINSON.
LEEDS, about 1770, ht. 5 in (12.75 cm)
Towner Collection. See page 132

59B TEAPOT, deep cream, enamelled in red and black by the Leeds firm of J. ROBINSON.
LEEDS, about 1770, ht. 5¼ in (13.3 cm)
Victoria and Albert Museum. See page 128

Rhodes,[1] but as already stated this firm also enamelled some of the wares of other potteries, notably Wedgwood, Cockpit Hill, Melbourne etc.

Glazes

The first glazes used by the Leeds Pottery were a soft, clear yellow, not the bright lemon-yellow of Cockpit Hill nor the yellowish-green of Wedgwood. Sometimes the Leeds glaze showed as a rich daffodil or buttercup yellow and sometimes tended towards a soft brown. Very occasionally a tendency to green occurs before 1775, but this is exceptional and almost certainly an accidental effect, the glaze having caught up some extraneous pigment or other glaze. The Leeds glazing was not generally so consistently uniform as the Wedgwood and although most of the Leeds creamware was uncrazed there was always a tendency for the glaze to craze where it ran thickly; when this occurred the mesh so formed was usually fairly regular and about one-eighth of an inch square. From about the year 1775 the Leeds glaze differed from the Wedgwood and most other Staffordshire glazes in being primrose-yellow in colour, though John Turner of Lane End, Staffordshire, used a very similar glaze at one time. Ware which received a full glaze appears very rich and creamy and is smooth to the touch. On the other hand, pieces which were more thinly glazed appear to be dry and chalky and feel somewhat rough. About 1780, a very soft greyish-green glaze was introduced. This was a much softer green than that used by Wedgwood, but very similar to a glaze used by the Yorkshire factory of Castleford. The glaze used by the Leeds Pottery on the elaborate chestnut-baskets (Plate 71A) and some other ware at this time was grey, sometimes tending towards green and occasionally towards blue. About 1780, an almost white body was introduced which has little to recommend it, and about 1790 the Leeds Pottery introduced a blue tinted glaze for the so-called 'pearlware'. The colour of this was a deep soft blue with no suggestion of green, differing in this respect from the pearlware of Wedgwood and other Staffordshire factories. Although it was usual in pearlware to use only just sufficient blue to counteract the cream colour, the Leeds blue was often deep enough to give the ware a decidedly bluish cast. This was the glaze used on most of the Leeds square-based figures. About 1800 a bright pale-green glaze was used for a few years only, and about 1820 a straw-coloured glaze was introduced for a rich buff-coloured ware very different from the early deep cream colour. Mention should also be made of a bright canary-yellow glaze which was introduced soon after 1800, but Leeds creamware of this colour is rare.[2]

---

[1] By the time the large new factory called The Leeds Pottery was built in 1770, the firm of Robinson and Rhodes was under the direction of Jasper Robinson, Rhodes having left in 1768. The firm was almost certainly known as J. Robinson and Co. from 1768–78 or 9, following its previous title of D. Rhodes and Co. from 1763–8.

[2] A pair of melon tureens covered with a bright yellow glaze and impressed 'LEEDS * POTTERY' are illustrated in *English Yellow-glazed Earthenware*, by J. Jefferson Miller II, London, 1974, Plate XXXVIII.

60   JUG, deep cream, enamelled in red and black. Inscribed 'Ale 1770'
Probably LEEDS, 1770, ht. 8¼ in (21 cm)
Formerly Towner Collection. See page 119

Forms and Details

The early Leeds creamware, that is to say, the deep cream-coloured ware made before the year 1775, consisted very largely of teapots, coffee-pots, punch-pots, jugs and mugs. Tea-services as such do not appear to have been made at this time. Even at a much later date, tea-, coffee- or chocolate-cups seem to have been made in small quantities only and to order, though cups and saucers more than any other type of ware have always been prone to breakage. Perhaps this may account for the extreme scarcity of creamware cups and saucers today. Punch-pots in the form of large teapots seem to have been in general use, some bearing the inscription 'Punch' painted upon them.

Types of form which became Leeds characteristics seem to be evident from the start of the factory. Teapots both 'square' and 'round' were made. These are the names given to straight-sided and globular teapots in the Leeds drawing books. Flower knobs were used for both tea- and coffee-pots, while double handles are general for jugs as well.

Much of the early Leeds creamware has a typical border pattern of a diagonally set 'bead-and-reel' moulded in relief (Plates 58A and 59B). This was superseded by the 'pearl' beading (Plates 64 and 65A). The handles, spouts, knobs and other details are discussed and illustrated in Appendix I.

Enamelling

The firm of Robinson and Rhodes inserted an advertisement in the *Leeds Intelligencer* for 28 October 1760, and another on 12 May 1761. The latter is quoted here as it is the rather fuller one:

ROBINSON and RHODES
Opposite the George in Briggate Leeds

ENAMEL and BURN in COLOURS and GOLD, Foreign and English CHINA; and match broken Sets of enamell'd China Tea Ware, with Foreign or English, and make them compleat to any Pattern requir'd, either *India* or *Dresden*. They also enamell Coats of Arms &c. and sell a good Assortment of Foreign China, and great Variety of useful English China, of the newest Improvement, which they engage to wear as well as Foreign, and will change gratis, if broke with hot Water. They also enamell Stone Ware, as cheap as in Staffordshire and sell all Sorts of fine Earthenware, Likewise, piece all Sorts of *India* Tea Ware, by melting it together in the Fire, so as to render it as useful, without revitting and to ring as well as before it was broken. Ready money or Goods for broken Flint Glass.

It should be remembered that the word 'China' at this time was used to denote either porcelain or earthenware and that 'Stoneware' was fine white saltglaze. David Rhodes was the senior partner of this firm. In 1763 Jasper Robinson surrendered his partnership and was employed by Rhodes in the firm, which then became D. Rhodes and Co. Rhodes, at this time, was corresponding with Wedgwood and in 1768 left for London, taking with him

E JUG, inscribed 'Ed. Clayton'. Enamelled by the Leeds firm of J. ROBINSON
YORKSHIRE, probably LEEDS, about 1770, ht. 8 in (20.3 cm)
Towner Collection. See page 132

F COFFEE-POT, painted in enamel colours by the Leeds firm of J. ROBINSON
YORKSHIRE, probably LEEDS, about 1770, ht. 9¾ in (24.8 cm)
Formerly Towner Collection. See page 132

On the jug: When / This you fee / Remember me / Tho many miles / We diftant be

61 JUG, deep cream, enamelled in red and black by the Leeds firm of J. ROBINSON.
Terminals touched with blue, green and yellow, green enamel edges
Probably HOLBECK, LEEDS, about 1768, ht. 9¾ in (24.8 cm)
Towner Collection. See page 132

62   COFFEE-POT, moderately deep cream, enamelled in soft red monochrome.
Terminals and knob touched with purple, green and yellow enamel. Underneath
are the incised initials 'J.D.' probably for Joseph Dennison of the Holbeck
Pottery, Leeds
Probably HOLBECK, LEEDS, about 1768, ht. 9¾ in (24.8 cm)
Towner Collection. See page 120

63 COFFEE-POT, deep cream, enamelled in red and black by the Leeds firm of J. ROBINSON. Terminals, knob and spout touched with blue, green and yellow enamel
Probably LEEDS, about 1773, ht. 9 in (22.8 cm)
Towner Collection. See page 132

an apprentice and another hand, and settled in St. Martin's Lane, moving the following year to Little China Row to work for Wedgwood as his master enameller until 1777, in which year he died (pages 52, 54, 58). After 1768, the firm at Leeds continued under Jasper Robinson till 1779, after which Leonard Hobson continued the business at 'the sign of the Golden Jarr in Briggate' till his death in 1799. A great deal of the enamelling on Leeds creamware was the work of Jasper Robinson and enamellers working under him who carried on the earlier tradition of Rhodes. A jug painted in polychrome colours with a north-country farmer on one side (Colour Plate E) and his farmhouse on the other and inscribed 'ED. CLAYTON', has all the appearance of being an early Leeds piece and therefore should not be dated earlier than 1770; it must consequently have been painted by the firm of J. Robinson although there is a striking similarity between the painting of the farmer and some of the figures painted by Rhodes on Wedgwood's creamware.

The enamelling of Robinson and Rhodes was freely executed, showing a fine vigour and stylization. At first it chiefly consisted of decoration in red and black only. Subjects which were most usual in these colours consisted of stylized flowers (Plate 59A), birds (Colour Plate F and Plates 63 and 65B), and landscapes, usually with a crossed tree (Plate 58A) and houses with very black smoke coming from the chimneys. A gate was often introduced as well as small clouds and birds. Figures, reminiscent of some saltglaze enamelling, either in red and black or in red only, were usual (Plate 58B), as well as inscriptions within a freely-painted cartouche of scroll-work in a fine convention (Plate 61). Another early style of painting which was done by this firm at Leeds consisted of flower painting in which a thick pink enamel was used with other colours such as red, green, yellow and blue, as well as some in red and black only, the leaves often ending in a corkscrew-like shape. At a slightly later date, a rosy purple was introduced which made a delightful and surprising clash with the bright orange-red which was such a feature of enamelling on creamware in general. Bands and stripes of these colours, sometimes with the addition of yellow and green, formed some original and good decoration (Colour Plate G), as well as landscapes in brilliant colours, which often included a building with an oversize weathercock. Some good painting in underglaze-blue was also done (Plate 73B). Besides the enamelling found on tea-ware, mention must be made of some good enamelling on dessert-ware (Plate 73A) and on screw-top boxes (Colour Plate H), probably for the dressing-table. Snuff-boxes, some of which were in the form of heads, were also enamelled and are an interesting class of creamware (Plate 74A). Leeds creamware, particularly plates, is often found with Dutch enamelling. This has a much drier look than the English; conspicuous on most of it is a purplish-brown colour (Plate 72B). Border patterns enamelled in the style of Wedgwood's Chelsea painted creamware, first appeared at Leeds towards the end of the eighteenth century (Plate 84).

64   COFFEE-POT, pale cream, enamelled in red monochrome
LEEDS, about 1775, ht. $9\frac{1}{4}$ in (23.5 cm)
City of Manchester Art Galleries. See page 128

65A   TEAPOT, pale cream, enamelled in red monochrome by the Leeds firm of J. ROBINSON.
LEEDS, about 1775, ht. 4½ in (11.5 cm)
Towner Collection. See page 128

65B   TEAPOT, pale cream, enamelled in red and black by the Leeds firm of J. ROBINSON, about 1775, ht. 4½ in (11.5 cm)
Towner Collection. See page 132

66A SUGAR-BOWL, pale cream, enamelled in crimson, terminals green
      LEEDS, about 1780, ht. 3¼ in (8.3 cm)
      Zeitlin Collection
66B TEAPOT, pale cream, enamelled in red, green, purple, yellow and black
      LEEDS, about 1780, ht. 3½ in (9 cm)
      Towner Collection

Colour-Glazed Wares

In the past this type of ware has been closely associated with the name of Thomas Whieldon, but it is now certain that it was made at Derby, Liverpool, Leeds and Melbourne as well as in Staffordshire, where it was made by Whieldon, Wedgwood and others. Quite a considerable proportion of this type of ware has unmistakable Leeds characteristics, such as the Leeds form of double intertwined handle and flower knob on teapots.

Much Leeds tortoiseshell ware has a dappled appearance (Plate 81), and a considerable amount of plain cream colour is often visible, especially on the underside of the object. The colours used were green, a brown which often tended towards pink or crimson, yellow, plum, and a grey which sometimes tended towards purple or green. The pots usually possess the Leeds characteristics of handles, spouts, knobs and details of mouldings (see Appendix I). If the tortoiseshell coffee-pot illustrated on Plate 82 be compared with that shown on Plate 67 it will be noticed that they both have the main characteristics of form and detail. Another type of creamware is decorated with vertical stripes of underglaze green (Plate 83A and B). Shards of this were found on the Whieldon site but these had a slightly browner tint of green than the Leeds ones, and although it was made at a number of factories, most of the ware of this type with which one is conversant is undoubtedly of Leeds origin. Both this class of ware and another which consists of reeded bands filled in with the green glaze are referred to and illustrated in a Leeds drawing book, and specimens marked 'LEEDS POTTERY' are also known. At Leeds the ware with vertical green stripes was made towards the end of the eighteenth century.

Transfer-Printing

It is uncertain when transfer-printing was first introduced at Leeds, but there is no doubt that decoration of this kind was done on a considerable scale at Leeds from about the year 1780. L. Jewitt, in *Ceramic Art of Great Britain* refers to the state of the Leeds Pottery in 1791, as follows: 'So great had the concern become that the yearly balance then struck amounted to over £51,500 and it is worth recording that in that year the value of the copper plates from which the transfer-printing was effected was £204.'

Of the colours used in the Leeds printing, the red was more orange in colour than in most of the prints by Sadler and Green on Wedgwood creamware. A plate with an abbey — probably Fountains Abbey — transfer-printed in red and marked 'Leeds Pottery' in the print is illustrated (Plate 79A). A purplish-black seems to have been peculiar to Leeds, and was often associated with a greenish-grey glaze which was sometimes crazed. The Victoria and Albert Museum coffee-pot, marked 'Leeds Pottery' in the print, is in this colour (Plate 78). Much of the Leeds printing was in jet black. The punch-kettle illustrated is a very fine example of this (Plate 79B). Other colours were used for Leeds transfer-printing from about the turn of the century, notably, light blue and sage green. From about 1818 light grey and sepia were used for the pottery's

67   COFFEE-POT, pale cream
      LEEDS, about 1780, ht. 8 in (20.3 cm)
      Formerly Gollancz Collection. See page 136

underglaze bat-printing. Printing in underglaze blue was first introduced at Leeds about 1810.

Among subjects which have been found with the Leeds Pottery mark in the print are the following:

    1 and 2. 'The Chariot of Love'. There are two versions of this subject, which sometimes occur on pieces which also bear the Leeds Pottery impressed mark.

    3 and 4. Bull-fighting scenes are printed in black on a coffee-pot in the Yorkshire Museum, which was probably intended for export to Spain.

    5. 'The Revd. John Wesley'.[1] The Leeds version of this subject differs from that which is sometimes signed 'Green Liverpool'.

    6. 'Love and Obedience'.[2]

    7. 'Faith'. These last three were probably printed for the Methodist Conferences held at Leeds in 1780.

    8. 'The Vicar and Moses' printed in jet black and washed over in enamel colours occurs on a jug in the Yorkshire Museum and is from an engraving by John Aynsley. The arms of Leeds, the golden fleece, are enamelled in front, also 'J.B.' and 'S.B.' above the words 'Success to the Leeds Manufactory'. The initials 'J.B.' and 'S.B.' probably refer to John Barwick, who was one of the partners of the Leeds Pottery in 1781, and his wife.[3]

    9. 'Arms of the Moderns' (Masonic).

    10. 'Fountains Abbey' (Plate 79A).

    11. 'Hagar and Ishmael'.

For notes on creamware printed in black and enamelled over with scenes from the story of 'The Prodigal Son', etc., see pages 40 and 150. Christopher Livesey, printer of Leeds, issued a trade card on which is inscribed 'Plates for Potteries, either Black or Blue Ware'. It seems likely that he may have been responsible for some of the transfer-printing on Leeds creamware. The trade card is illustrated in the catalogue of *Creamware and Other English Pottery at Temple Newsam House*, by Peter Walton (Leeds, 1976).

Pierced Decoration

An enormous amount of plain useful creamware was made at the Leeds Pottery. This is generally of fine form but not so light in weight as the more delicate pieces, as it was often made thicker in order to stand up to more general usage. The lists published with the Leeds pattern book[4] give an idea of the extraordinary variety of utilitarian creamware made. The ware, however, for

[1] Illustrated in Donald C. Towner, *Handbook of Leeds Pottery*, Leeds, 1951, p. 44.
[2] As note 1.
[3] Illustrated in O. Grabham, *Yorkshire Potteries, Pots and Potters*, York, 1916, p. 58; and in A. Hurst, *Catalogue of the Boynton Collection*, York, 1922, p. 62.
[4] These lists, of which the originals are very rare, were reproduced by J. and F. Kidson in *Historical Notices of the Leeds Old Pottery*, Leeds, 1892, pp. 33–34, and in Donald Towner, *The Leeds Pottery*, London, 1963.

68　PUNCH-KETTLE and STAND, pale cream
LEEDS, about 1775, ht. of kettle $8\frac{3}{4}$ in (22.3 cm), ht. of stand $5\frac{7}{8}$ in (15 cm)
Leeds Art Galleries

which the Leeds Pottery is particularly famed is creamware with pierced open-work decoration (Plates 71A, B and 72A), and the elaborate centre-pieces (Plates 69 and 70). These last were an extraordinary feat of technical achievement. Chestnut-baskets with elaborately pierced sides and cover are sometimes marked 'LEEDS * POTTERY' or 'HARTLEY GREENS & CO.' (see Appendix III). Twig-baskets and dishes of basket-work pattern were made in quantities for dessert; these were somewhat similar to those made by other factories though many made at Leeds were characterized by having a plain centre.

69   CENTRE-PIECE, pale cream
      LEEDS, about 1780, ht. 24 in (61 cm)
      Colonial Williamsburg Foundation. See page 139

70   CENTRE-PIECE, pale cream
      LEEDS, about 1780, ht. 25 in (63.5 cm)
      Fitzwilliam Museum, Cambridge. See page 139

71A   CHESTNUT-BASKET and STAND, pale cream
       LEEDS, about 1780, ht. 8⅝ in (21.9 cm)
       Victoria and Albert Museum. See pages 126 and 139
71B   TEAPOT, deep cream
       LEEDS, about 1775, ht. 5¼ in (13.5 cm)
       Leeds Art Galleries. See page 139

72A PLATE, pale cream. Portrait of the first Duke of Marlborough, after Kneller,
enamelled in sepia. Other decoration in purple and gold
LEEDS, about 1780, diam. 9¾ in (24.8 cm)
Formerly Towner Collection. See page 139

72B PLATE, pale cream, enamelled in red, brown, green, yellow, blue and black, in
Holland, with portraits of Prince William V of Orange and his Princess on the
occasion of their return from exile in 1787. Inscribed in black with loyal
acclamations
LEEDS, 1787, diam. 9½ in (24.2 cm)
Zeitlin Collection. See page 132

73A   TUREEN, shaped as a melon, pale cream, enamelled in purple, crimson, yellow and green
      LEEDS, about 1780, ht. 5 in (12.2 cm)
      Leeds Art Galleries. See page 132

73B   TUREEN, pale cream, painted in underglaze-blue
      LEEDS, about 1780, ht. $9\frac{1}{4}$ in (23.5 cm), length 14 in (35.5 cm)
      Towner Collection. See page 132

74A SNUFF-BOXES as heads, with screw-on bases, pale cream: (i) decorated with purplish manganese and green underglaze colours; (ii) enamelled in pink, blue, red, green and yellow; (iii) enamelled in plum, green, blue, grey and flesh; (iv) painted in underglaze-blue
LEEDS, 1780–90, ht. 3½ in (9 cm)
Formerly Gollancz Collection. See page 132

74B CUP and SAUCER, pale cream, enamelled in red, purple, green, yellow and black
LEEDS, about 1775, ht. of cup 2 in (5.1 cm), diam. of saucer 5 in (12.7 cm)
Towner Collection

Figures

It is not usually realized that the Leeds Pottery produced figures decorated with coloured glazes in the style that is so much associated with the name of Thomas Whieldon, but such is the case. A group in the Victoria and Albert Museum (Plate 75) in this type of colouring is further decorated by the application of eleven flowers from a single mould; these flowers being the upper portion of the particular form of flower knob used by the Leeds Pottery for teapots (see Appendix I, Plate VII:4c). The style of head-dress worn by the lady in this group was first introduced about 1770. The date of this piece could therefore be placed a few years later. An almost identical group is in the Colonial Williamsburg Collection, while a very similar group, but without the applied flowers, in the Willett Collection at Brighton, is in saltglaze. The slight differences of costume suggest that the saltglaze group was an earlier model.

Animals and birds were also made at Leeds, some of them being decorated with a soft grass-green glaze often with additional touches of grey or yellow. A number of figures and animals, however, were also made in the same brilliant rich creamware but were left uncoloured. The best Leeds figures both of this type and that which succeeded it, namely the 'square-base' figures, are very pleasing. The modeller for the most part chose very intimate homely subjects and endowed them with character. Most of the female figures seem to represent the same young woman, who though slightly snub-nosed and possessing a receding chin has great charm (Plate 76). The classical figures though good are rather less interesting. One or two of the old moulds survived the factory, and figures have been made from these in modern times and impressed 'LEEDS. POTTERY'. Such figures are more grey in appearance and the glaze on them is usually crazed. The brilliance of the original creamware never seems to have been successfully imitated.

Certain characteristics may be noted in attempting to identify the Leeds figures. The figures are completely open underneath (that is to say that on turning the piece upside-down, one can see the whole of the interior). The only exceptions to this rule are the few copies made at Leeds of figures which originated at other factories. Most of the figures with square bases are of pearlware, with an extremely smooth and brilliant heavy blue glaze, free from any tinge of green. This glaze often gives the figures a distinct bluish cast. The base itself is deeper than that of the Staffordshire square-base figures, and a nick is often discernible inside the corners. This was deliberately made with a pointed tool to prevent the development of fire-cracks. The enamel colours include a clear sea-green, orange, pinkish mauve, pale yellow and black. Full use was made of spots as a form of enamel decoration.

Certain Leeds figures such as Sir Isaac Newton are variations on those by Ralph Wood.

The following is a short list of some of the Leeds figures which are known to have been marked with the original Leeds Pottery impressed mark:

75   GROUP, pale cream, decorated with green and brown glazes (cf. applied flowers
      with Leeds flower knob, Appendix I, Plate VII:4c)
      LEEDS, about 1775, ht. 7½ in (19 cm)
      Victoria and Albert Museum. See page 146

76   FIGURE, from a pair of FALCONERS, pearlware, enamelled in yellow, dark red,
      turquoise, brown and black. Mark 'LEEDS POTTERY.' impressed
      LEEDS, about 1785, ht. 7½ in (19 cm)
      British Museum. See pages 146 and 150

77 FIGURES, PAIR OF STREET-MUSICIANS, pale cream
LEEDS, about 1785, ht. 7½ in (18.5 cm)
Walford Collection. See page 150

Late Wares

During the early years of the nineteenth century many new types of ware were introduced by the Leeds Pottery. About 1800 a creamware that had a slightly grey appearance and was very light in weight was made. It was decorated with formal designs and sprigs in underglaze mineral colours of brown, deep blue, sage-green and orange-buff. This class of ware is usually associated with Pratt of Fenton, but was also made at Bristol and elsewhere. By about 1810 the Leeds Pottery, in common with a number of others, was producing marbled creamware in tones of black, brown, brownish-red and cream. Leeds examples of this ware as well as of a buff-coloured ware frequently consisted of mugs and teapots decorated with moulded swags and portrait medallions of Admiral Keppel, Lord Nelson and others (Plate 85B(i)). After 1810, the Leeds Pottery added to its production numerous types of simple band and check patterns. These included vertical bands of black or dark brown, small chequered patterns in black or pale blue (Plate 85B(ii)), and broad horizontal bands of orange-buff (Plate 85B(iii)), the contrasting colour in each case being cream. This type of decoration was made by most creamware factories of the time. In addition, creamware with enamelled formal border patterns in the style of Wedgwood was produced (Plate 84), as well as dessert-services painted with named flowers copied from illustrations in botanical books, lustreware (chiefly silver), and a very deep buff-coloured ware decorated with monochrome painted landscapes or with holly and ivy leaves in dark green (Plate 85A) and underglaze transfer-printed wares, as well as the yellow-glazed ware already mentioned.

A number of figures of horses about sixteen inches high, said to have been made for display in the windows of corn-chandlers' shops, were made in the vicinity of Leeds soon after 1800. These are inferior in both body and glaze to the best creamware of the Leeds Pottery. A horse of this kind in the Yorkshire Museum has the letters 'L.P.' enamelled on a corner of the saddle-cloth.

There has been a great deal of uncertainty regarding the origin of a large group of creamware teapots made about 1780, either painted in enamels with subjects such as 'Aurora' (Plate 80A) or transfer-printed in black and enamelled over with such subjects as 'The Prodigal Son' (Plate 36A). There is no doubt that some of these teapots were made at Leeds—Plate 80B shows a probable example—but the whole group is discussed in Chapter 2 under 'William Greatbatch'.

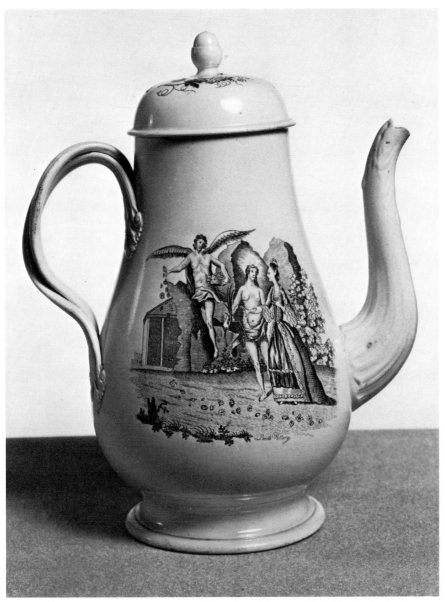

78   COFFEE-POT, pale cream, transfer-printed in purplish black, depicting two
allegories. Mark 'Leeds Pottery' in the print
LEEDS, about 1785, ht. 9 in (22.7 cm)
Victoria and Albert Museum. See page 136

79A PLATE, pale cream, transfer-printed in red with a ruined abbey, probably
Fountains Abbey. Mark 'Leeds Pottery' inscribed in the print
LEEDS, about 1780, diam. 9⅞ in (25.2 cm)
Formerly Towner Collection. See page 136

79B PUNCH-KETTLE, pale cream, transfer-printed in black with 'May Day'; on the
reverse 'Harlequin and Columbine'; butterflies on the cover
LEEDS, about 1780, ht. 8¼ in (21 cm)
Formerly Gollancz Collection. See page 136

80A   TEAPOT, pale cream, enamelled in red, green, purple, yellow and black with 'Aurora'; on the reverse the rising sun between two cherubs
Probably LEEDS, about 1780, ht. 5¾ in (14.7 cm)
Formerly Towner Collection. See pages 40 and 150

80B   TEAPOT, pale cream, transfer-printed and enamelled in red, green, purple, yellow and black with 'The Fortune Teller' by WILLIAM GREATBATCH
Probably LEEDS, about 1778, ht. 5¼ in (13 cm)
Leeds Art Galleries. See pages 40 and 150

81   CHOCOLATE-POT, pale cream, mottled with purplish-grey manganese
LEEDS, about 1775, ht. 4½ in (11.5 cm)
Victoria and Albert Museum. See page 136

82   COFFEE-POT, pale cream, mottled with brown manganese
      LEEDS, about 1775, ht. $9\frac{7}{8}$ in (25.2 cm)
      Leeds Art Galleries. See page 136

83A   TEAPOT, pale cream, decorated with stripes of green glaze
         LEEDS, about 1780, ht. 4⅞ in (12.5 cm)
         Victoria and Albert Museum. See page 136

83B   (i) PAIR OF EGG-CUPS, pearlware, edged with green glaze
         LEEDS, about 1785, ht. 2¾ in (7 cm)
         (ii) CREAM-JUG, pale cream, decorated with stripes of green glaze
         LEEDS, about 1785, ht. 3 in (7.6 cm)
         Formerly Towner Collection. See page 136

84   CHOCOLATE-JUG and STAND, pearlware, enamelled in brown and purple. 'GFK'
inscribed in monogram. Mark 'LEEDS * POTTERY' impressed
LEEDS, about 1790, ht. of jug 5 in (12.7 cm), length of stand 6½ in (16.5 cm)
Formerly Gollancz Collection. See pages 132 and 150

85A   SAUCE-TUREEN, STAND and LADLE, buff-coloured ware, decorated with dark green enamel and gold lustre. Mark 'HARTLEY GREENS AND CO. LEEDS * POTTERY' impressed twice crossing each other
Leeds, about 1819, length of stand 7½ in (19 cm)
Leeds Art Galleries. See page 150

85B   (i) TEAPOT, pale cream, coloured slips of red and black, touches of green glaze, with a portrait of Rodney in relief
Leeds, about 1790, ht. 3 in (7.6 cm)
(ii) TEACUP and SAUCER, pearlware, inlay simulating granite, black and white chequered border
Leeds, about 1805, diam. of saucer 4¼ in (10.7 cm)
(iii) TEAPOT, pale cream, decorated in black and cinnamon slips. Mark 'LEEDS * POTTERY' impressed
Leeds, about 1805, ht. 6½ in (16.5 cm)
Victoria and Albert Museum. See page 150

Pattern and Drawing Books

Pattern books were issued by a number of leading potteries in England. They were catalogues with engraved illustrations and descriptive lists of the wares in current production for the guidance of wholesale or retail traders in England or abroad in placing their orders. The first Leeds Pottery pattern book was published in 1783. Books of working drawings for use in the Leeds Pottery itself have been preserved. Three of these are at the Victoria and Albert Museum and nine others at the Leeds City Art Galleries. Both these and the pattern books are discussed in Appendix II.

Marks

Only a very small proportion of Leeds creamware made before 1800 was marked. It is possible that the Leeds Pottery only marked those pieces which were destined for other factories for resale or by special request. A frequently repeated note in the Leeds order books is: 'Ordered at Swinton, to be marked etc.' The most usual Leeds Pottery mark consists of the words 'LEEDS * POTTERY' in capital letters, impressed, with an asterisk between the two words. An impressed mark consisting of the two words 'LEEDS POTTERY', without the asterisk but often with a full stop instead, has been used on creamware of recent manufacture. It must be pointed out however that the Leeds Pottery mark with the full stop was also an authentic mark used from about 1800. These marks have caused a great deal of confusion amongst those who are not intimate with the original creamware of the Leeds Pottery. Not only are modern pieces which bear the Leeds Pottery mark often bought in the belief that they are the products of the original factory, but collectors and others who have been disillusioned in this respect, often refuse to buy original Leeds creamware because it is so marked and therefore likely to be modern.

For illustrations of the Leeds Pottery marks with notes, see Appendix III.

Excavations of the Leeds Pottery site now taking place (1977) so far confirm the attributions to that pottery made in this book.

Chapter 8

OTHER YORKSHIRE POTTERIES

SWINTON

Two potteries existed at Swinton in Yorkshire in the eighteenth century, namely the Swinton Pottery and the Don Pottery.

Swinton lies in the south of Yorkshire, eleven miles north-east of Sheffield. The Swinton Pottery was established in 1745 by Edward Butler. In 1763 it came into the hands of William Malpass who was joined by William Fenney from the Rotherham Pottery in 1767 or 1768. John Brameld became a partner with his two sons, William and Thomas; it is uncertain when their partnerships began, but William started work at the pottery in 1786 and Thomas in 1795. In 1778 Thomas Bingley became a partner with Malpass and the pottery traded under the name Thomas Bingley and Co. In 1785 it became associated with the Leeds Pottery and traded under the name Greens, Bingley and Co., and sometime prior to 1796 Greens, Hartley and Co., John and Joshua Green and William Hartley being the principal partners of both potteries. This association ended in 1806 and the firm continued under the name Brameld and Co. until 1825 or 1826 when it was renamed the Rockingham Works.

Jewitt states that the first ware to be made under Edward Butler was a hard brownware. This was undoubtedly brown salt-glazed stoneware. He illustrates a two-handled loving-cup dated 1759 which is clearly of this ware and is authenticated as having been made at the Swinton Pottery. It would seem that fine white saltglaze was made at Swinton at an early date as well as tortoiseshell ware and a ware covered with a fine green glaze. Pieces of this last sometimes bear the impressed mark 'BRAMELD' (Appendix III: 85 and 86) and are from the same moulds as some white salt-glazed stoneware. The Swinton Pottery issued pattern books. The first of these had the following heading:

> Greens, Bingley & Co., Swinton Pottery, make, sell, and export wholesale all sorts of Earthenware, Cream Coloured or Queen's, Nankeen Blue, Tortoiseshell, Fine Egyptian Black, Brown, China etc. etc. All the above sorts enamelled, printed or ornamented with gold or silver.

G TEAPOT, painted in enamel colours
LEEDS, about 1775, ht. $4\frac{3}{4}$ in (12.2 cm)
Formerly Towner Collection. See page 132

H SCREW-TOP BOXES. Top left, painted at Derby, probably MELBOURNE
Bottom right, probably WEDGWOOD, about 1775, diam. 3 in (7.6 cm)
Towner Collection. See page 132

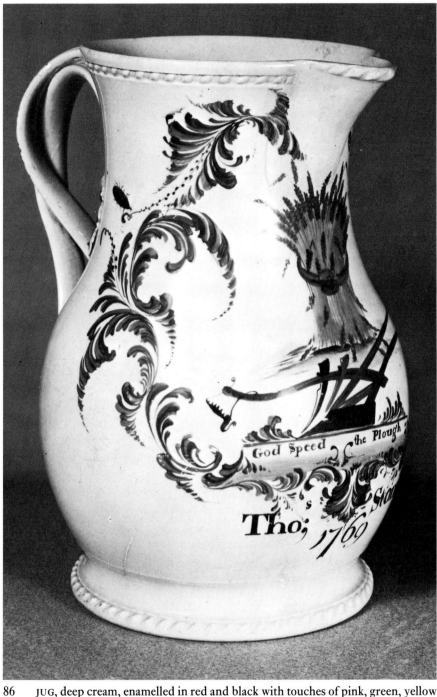

86   JUG, deep cream, enamelled in red and black with touches of pink, green, yellow
and blue on terminals. Inscribed 'Thos; Stonier 1769'
YORKSHIRE, 1769, ht. 7½ in (19 cm)
Victoria and Albert Museum. See pages 120 and 124

A second pattern book with the heading 'Greens, Hartley & Co.', has on the flyleaf an announcement of an increase in prices and a revised system of numbering. It is dated 'Swinton Pottery, 1st February 1796'.

In many instances the designs in the Leeds and Swinton pattern books are similar and it would seem that the Leeds Pottery kept Swinton supplied with creamware when the latter's stocks were low, as we find in a Leeds account book a number of entries with the words, 'Ordered to Swinton and there accred. to be marked'.

Very little is known of the Swinton creamware of the eighteenth century. Marked pieces are rare but show that the quality was good, though less fine than that of the Leeds creamware, and that it was very light in weight. The mark 'BRAMELD' is occasionally found impressed on creamware.

DON POTTERY

This pottery which was situated close to the canal at Swinton was founded in 1801[1] by John Green, formerly of the Leeds Pottery, Richard Clark and John and William Brameld. By 1803, John Green's son John, William Clark, John Milner and John Wade had become partners. John Green senior died in 1805 and William Green, his second son, became a partner. This pottery became the largest creamware factory in Yorkshire after the Leeds Pottery. It continued to work until 1893. In 1807 the pottery traded under the name Green, Clark and Co., and from 1816 John and William Green and Co., or Greens and Co. John and William Green were bankrupt in 1834. In 1839 it was bought by Samuel Barker. In 1808 the Don Pottery issued a pattern book very similar to the Leeds Pottery one, but containing more engraved designs. The creamware produced was inferior to that of the Leeds Pottery and often showed crazing and a lack of finish. Botanical flower paintings on a whitish creamware were amongst its best productions. Other types of ware made by the Don Pottery include: transfer-printed creamware, underglaze-blue printed ware, green-glazed ware, buff-coloured ware, black basalt stoneware, open-work creamware baskets, tureens etc., and pearlware. The marks used on the creamware of this factory are illustrated in Appendix III: 87 to 90.

CASTLEFORD

Castleford is three miles north of Pontefract at the junction of the rivers Calder and Aire. The first fine-ware pottery was built by William Taylor in 1786. In 1790 it was bought by David Dunderdale and John Plowes. Though much of

[1] 1790 is the date given by both Jewitt and Kidson for the foundation of the Don Pottery, but Hurst in his *Boynton Collection Catalogue* states that the *Directory* of 1833 gives the date 1801 for the first establishment of the pottery. This date has now been confirmed by Heather Lawrence.

87 JUG, deep cream
ROTHWELL, YORKSHIRE, about 1770, ht. 5⅝ in (14.3 cm)
Towner Collection. See page 164

the earlier creamware was good, it was generally inferior to that of the Leeds Pottery. A rather heavy greyish-green glaze is characteristic. The Castleford Pottery issued a pattern book in 1796 clearly based on the Leeds one. It shows the very great variety of ware produced by this pottery. Perhaps one of the most striking differences between the wares of Castleford and Leeds as seen in the pattern books is that where a piece is surmounted by a flower knob at Leeds, in the Castleford pattern book its place is taken by an onion-shaped knob. Although handles in the Castleford pattern book clearly follow a late Leeds pattern some of those seen on actual marked pieces have been clearly derived from Wedgwood designs. The ware for which this factory was famed was white felspathic stoneware, of which the well-known moulded teapots edged with blue enamel were made, although it must be pointed out that the Castleford Pottery was by no means the only factory to produce this type of ware. The marks used are illustrated in Appendix III:91 and 92. A fine quality creamware plate with a neat border pattern and the impressed mark 'D.D. & CO. CASTLEFORD' is illustrated (Plate 89B).

ROTHWELL

Rothwell is about four miles south-east of Leeds. The pottery was founded in 1768 when it was being worked by John Smith and Co. On 19 May 1770 Smith was advertising for the sale of a one-third share of the pot-works. Further advertisements for the sale of the pottery appear in the *Leeds Mercury* for 13 April 1773 and 3 May 1774. These show that there was still remaining to the pottery three kilns, two large warehouses and other 'convenient houses for carrying on the pottery business in the most commodious and extensive manner', a flint mill, 'a dwelling house for the grinder and 3 spacious rooms, well lighted and fitted up for Enamel work', all of which suggests a pottery of some importance. It would seem that the Leeds Pottery bought much of the stock and that the Rothwell Pottery was then being worked by William Taylor and in 1785 by Elizabeth Medley who ran it for a few years longer. Shards recently found on the pottery site show that a number of different types of ware were made here which include white saltglaze, green-glazed wares and a good quality creamware (Plate 87), some with tortoiseshell decoration of very small touches of crimson and rich green on a yellowish creamware ground, which is very distinctive (Plate 88A). Various moulded borders for plates were also found. These are illustrated in Appendix I, Plate XI:1, 2 and 3.

On 21 June 1774 the following advertisement appeared in the *Leeds Mercury*: 'A New Pottery. This is to inform the public that Samuel Shaw of Rothwell, potter (late from Staffordshire), makes and sells all sorts of cream colour, red, yellow and painted wares at his new pottery in Rothwell. . . .' The date of this advertisement corresponds so well with the sale of the Rothwell Pottery, that one would assume that it was bought by Shaw. This, however, does not seem to have been the case but it would appear that Shaw started a second pottery in Rothwell. Shaw died in 1776, when on the 23 July the following advertisement appeared in the *Leeds Mercury*: 'To be sold, By Wholesale or Retail at the House of the late Samuel Shaw, in Rothwell, deceased. All sorts of Cream-coloured and Painted Earthenware, also all kinds of coarse ware. The House, Workhouse and all Tools and Implements belonging to the Pottery to be lett.' The red and yellow wares mentioned were presumably the glazed earthenware of the so-called Astbury type.

88A   TEAPOT, deep cream, mottled with rich green and crimson manganese, some
      gilding
      ROTHWELL, YORKSHIRE, about 1770, ht. 5½ in (14 cm)
      Victoria and Albert Museum. See page 164
88B   SUGAR-BOWL, whiteware, painted in high temperature mineral colours of blue,
      yellow, green and brown. Mark 'FERRYBRIDGE' impressed
      FERRYBRIDGE, YORKSHIRE, about 1805, ht. 4¼ in (10.8 cm)
      Victoria and Albert Museum. See page 166

FERRYBRIDGE

Prior to 1804, known as the Knottingley Pottery

Pot-works were established here in 1793 by William Tomlinson and others and traded under Tomlinson, Foster and Company. In June 1798, Ralph Wedgwood, a nephew of Josiah Wedgwood, was taken into partnership and the pottery traded under Tomlinson, Foster, Wedgwood and Company, but in January 1801 Ralph Wedgwood was bought out on account of the many breakages caused by his experiments. The firm was then styled William Tomlinson and Company. After many vicissitudes and changes of ownership the pottery is still working as Thomas Brown and Sons Ltd. A 'Shape and Pattern Book' with the heading 'W. & Co. Ferrybridge' which can be dated as 1799 is in the Wedgwood archives. Ralph Wedgwood was formerly at the Hillworks, Burslem, but the mark 'WEDGWOOD & CO' should be associated with the Ferrybridge Pottery. Some good quality creamware in imitation of Wedgwood's Queen's ware was made at Ferrybridge. Other wares include pearlware, marbled ware, blackware, etc. The marks used by the Ferrybridge Pottery are illustrated in Appendix III:94 and 95. A sugar-basin and cover with the impressed mark 'FERRYBRIDGE' is illustrated (Plate 88B).

HUNSLET HALL

This pottery was founded in 1800 by Samuel Rainforth, between five and six hundred yards south-west of the Leeds Pottery. It was first styled Rainforth and Co., and pieces that have come under notice were so impressed. Such pieces were either painted in high temperature mineral colours (Plate 89A) or printed in underglaze blue, but if they can be taken as typical examples, the ware which was whitish and not true creamware was very inferior to that of the Leeds Pottery. Rainforth died in 1817. In 1818 the firm was Petty and Co. There were various succeeding owners before the pottery was finally closed in 1881. (For mark used see Appendix III:93).

ROTHERHAM

This pottery was founded in 1765 by John Platt and William Fenney. The partnership lasted less than a year and from 1766 John Platt was in partnership with Samuel Walker junior. In 1772 Platt and Walker sold the pottery to Samuel Walker senior, who in 1777 was joined by William Hawley. It is thought that production ceased about 1800. Platt and Walker issued a trade

89A PLATE, pearlware, painted in blue, green, brown and yellow high temperature
     mineral colours. Impressed mark 'RAINFORTH & CO.'
     HUNSLET HALL POTTERY, YORKSHIRE, about 1805, diam. $7\frac{1}{2}$ in (19.1 cm)
     Victoria and Albert Museum. See page 166
89B PLATE, pale cream, enamelled in brown. Impressed mark 'D.D. & CO.
     CASTLEFORD'
     CASTLEFORD, YORKSHIRE, about 1800, diam. $8\frac{1}{2}$ in (21.6 cm)
     Victoria and Albert Museum. See page 164

card stating that they made 'White Stoneware' (saltglaze), 'Black, Tortoise-shell, Agate, Cream Colour etc. also Gilt and Enamel Ware for Tea and Table Services' (see *E.E.C. Transactions*, Vol. 5, Part 3, 1962, Plate 168).

A saltglaze jug inscribed 'John Platt 1767' can be ascribed to this pottery with confidence (see *E.C.C. Transactions*, Vol. 9, Part 1, 1973, Plates 64 and 65).

BELLE VUE POTTERY, HULL

This pottery was founded in 1802 by James and Jeremiah Smith of Hull, Job Ridgway of Shelton, Staffordshire, and Josiah Hipwood of Hull. In 1806 the sole proprietors were Job and George Ridgway, and in 1826 the pottery passed into the hands of William Bell. The pottery was closed in 1841.

The creamware made at the Belle Vue Pottery was very inferior to the best quality creamware. It was clumsily potted and the glaze was usually crazed. Plates with a ship transfer-printed in black upon them are sometimes found with the impressed mark of two bells on the back. The factory mark is illustrated in Appendix III:97.

STAFFORD POTTERY, STOCKTON-ON-TEES

This pottery, which was established in 1824 or 1825 by William Smith, was situated on the Yorkshire side of the River Tees at Thornaby. It is of interest to collectors of eighteenth-century creamware chiefly on account of its mark, which sometimes consisted of the word 'WEDGWOOD', or 'WEDGEWOOD' (see Appendix III:96, 98, 99 and 100). An injunction restraining the Stafford Pottery from using these marks was granted to the firm of Wedgwood of Etruria in 1848.[1] The wares produced by the Stafford Pottery are stated by Hurst in *A Catalogue of the Boynton Collection of Yorkshire Pottery* to have been 'good ordinary wares for domestic use'.

SWILLINGTON BRIDGE POTTERY

This was situated on the river Aire at Woodlesford, about five miles south-east of Leeds. It was built in 1791 by William Taylor who was bankrupt in 1795. After several other ownerships, by 1817 it was trading as Wildblood and Co. Oxley Grabham in *Yorkshire Potteries, Pots and Potters* records that a round creamware plaque with figures in relief and painted in enamel colours, has incised on the back, 'John Wildblood Swillington Bridge Pottery, July 12th, 1831'. It may be that many unidentified plaques of this nature are of

---

[1] A full account of this is given in the *Leeds Intelligencer* of 2 December 1848.

Swillington Bridge creamware. A crown impressed is said to be a mark of this factory.

At the beginning of the eighteenth century many small potteries were started in Yorkshire. Very few of these produced creamware of any quality and they are beyond the scope of this book. For fuller information about them the reader is recommended to read *Yorkshire Pots and Potteries* by Heather Lawrence (1974).

Chapter 9

LIVERPOOL AND OTHER CREAMWARE FACTORIES

At present our knowledge of Liverpool creamware is practically limited to that made by the Herculaneum Pottery which was not founded till 1796. That there were earlier creamware factories in Liverpool there is no doubt as there are various references to them. For instance, an advertisement for the sale of the 'Flint Potworks' after the death of J. Okill the proprietor in 1773 states that part of the stock-in-trade consisted of 'cream colour or Queensware, manufactured at the said works, which is now carried on in great perfection'. These works were taken over by Rigg and Peacock in 1774 'where they intend carrying on the business of making all kinds of cream-coloured earthenware' and according to Mayer it was being carried on by John Sykes and Co. well into the 1790s, but no creamware is so far attributable to them. Other Liverpool potters reputed to have manufactured creamware were: Seth Pennington at Shaw's Brow from about 1778 to 1805, Zachariah Barnes at 'The Haymarket Pottery', and Philip Christian at Shaw's Brow where Mayer tells us he made tortoiseshell ware of the Whieldon type. Even with such men as Richard Abbey and Joseph Johnson whose signatures we are familiar with on transfer-printed pieces (Plate 90A and B), it is difficult to be certain of the full part played by them in the Liverpool pottery trade.

RICHARD ABBEY

Richard Abbey was born in 1754 and was apprenticed to Sadler and Green, a firm of Liverpool transfer-printers, in 1767. In 1773 he set up on his own in Clieveland Square, Liverpool, where according to an advertisement in the *Liverpool Advertiser* of 19 December 1773 he both made and printed creamware. This reads as follows:

> Richard Abbey. Late Apprentice to Messrs. Sadler and Green Begs leave to inform his Friends and the Public that he has Open'd his Shop, at No. 11, in Clieveland Square, where he manufactures and Sells all sorts of Queen's

90A TEAPOT, pale cream, transfer-printed in reddish-brown from an engraving by
RICHARD ABBEY. Mark 'Abbey' in the print
LIVERPOOL, about 1795, ht. 6½ in (16.5 cm)
Fitzwilliam Museum, Cambridge. See pages 170 and 172

90B TEAPOT, pearlware, transfer-printed in rose-pink with 'L'Amour', on both sides
HERCULANEUM factory, LIVERPOOL, about 1800, ht. 5¼ in (13.4 cm)
Victoria and Albert Museum. See pages 170 and 174

Ware, Printed in the neatest Manner, and in a Variety of Colours. N.B. Orders for Exportation Also Crests, Coats of Arms, Tiles or any other particular Device will be completed at the shortest Notice By their most obedient humble Servant Richard Abbey.

Mayer states that in 1794 Abbey took the old copper works in Toxteth for the manufacture of creamware. This was the site acquired two years later by Samuel Worthington for the establishment of the Herculaneum Pottery. There is little doubt that Abbey should be considered first and foremost as a free-lance engraver of prints for the decoration of pottery and we are familiar with his signature 'R. Abbey Sculpt' which occurs on wares so decorated by him, sometimes in conjunction with other names such as Joseph Johnson, who seems to have been a pottery printer and perhaps made a certain amount of creamware as well in or near Liverpool. A creamware teapot at the Fitzwilliam Museum whose forms differ from those associated with Leeds or Staffordshire bears the inscription 'R. Abbey, Liverpool', in the print (Plate 90A), and is probably of Liverpool manufacture.

SADLER AND GREEN

Sadler and Green were printing tiles at Liverpool in 1756. In 1761 John Sadler entered into an agreement with Josiah Wedgwood that he should buy creamware ready glazed from him and sell it back when it had been printed on. This arrangement had obvious drawbacks and a fresh agreement was made in 1763 whereby Sadler should charge Wedgwood for the printing only. It was further agreed that Wedgwood should supply Sadler with all the ware he needed for his business. As a result, it would be largely true to say that all the transfer-printing on Wedgwood's creamware was done by Sadler and Green, the latter having been taken into partnership with Sadler in 1761, and except for a few instances when Sadler had none of Wedgwood's creamware and had to buy from other local potters to keep working, all creamware printed by Sadler was Wedgwood's. This agreement was very largely adhered to. Although the names Sadler and Green appear on some of the prints, they were not engravers, but printers only. They employed such men as John Evans, Thomas Billinge and Richard Abbey who were outside engravers. The various prints and colours used by Sadler and Green on Wedgwood's creamware will be found in Chapter 3 of this book.

Besides transfer-printing, Sadler and Green also decorated in enamel colours to a limited extent. Sadler retired from business in 1770, after which the firm was in the hands of Guy Green till 1799 when he too retired. Examples of printing by Sadler and Green will be found illustrated on Plates 10, 11, 21, 22, 23A and 25.

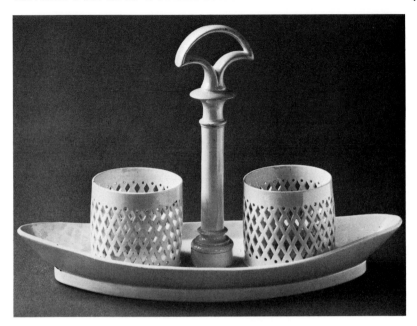

91A   CRUET-STAND, pale cream. Impressed mark 'HERCULANEUM'
      HERCULANEUM factory, LIVERPOOL, about 1810, ht. 6⅝ in (16.8 cm), length 10½
      in (26.6 cm)
      Manchester City Art Gallery. See page 174
91B   DISH, pale cream, painted with a landscape in natural colours, the border in
      yellowish-green and crimson
      HERCULANEUM factory, LIVERPOOL, about 1810, width 8 in (20.2 cm)
      Victoria and Albert Museum. See page 174

HERCULANEUM

When in 1793 or 1794 Richard Abbey, the engraver, founded a pottery on the south shore of the Mersey at Toxteth Park for the manufacture of creamware, he took a potter named Graham into partnership, but sold the factory in 1796 to Worthington, Humble and Holland, who named the factory 'Herculaneum'.

The creamware made at the Herculaneum factory is generally inferior in quality to the best creamware, though occasionally pieces with the impressed mark 'HERCULANEUM' (Appendix III: 140) are found which are of a very high standard (Plate 91A). Some good early pieces which are almost certainly from this factory have blue enamelled borders and rose-pink transfer-printing. The teapot illustrated (Plate 90B) is transfer-printed in rose-pink on pearlware, but Herculaneum pieces of fine quality creamware transfer-printed in this colour are known. Some good enamelling, particularly of landscapes, sometimes occurs on marked pieces (Plate 91B), but this type of decoration was soon superseded by blue-printing, black underglaze printing and bat-printing.

An enormous number of large size jugs and bowls transfer-printed with ships and various other subjects that would appeal to sailors were made for the Liverpool market. These were mostly printed at Liverpool and no doubt a great many were made by the Herculaneum Pottery, but as they were hardly ever marked it is very difficult to make attributions. From the turn of the century the usual chequered and banded slip-decorated ware was produced. In 1833 the factory traded under the name Case, Mort and Co. and in 1841 it was finally closed.

NEWCASTLE-UPON-TYNE

A group of potteries were founded in Newcastle and its district during the eighteenth and early nineteenth centuries. The first of these is said to have been established between 1730 and 1740 at Carr's Hill Pottery near Gateshead, where white salt-glazed stoneware was apparently made.[1] The most important creamware factory in the neighbourhood of Newcastle was at St. Anthony's, and was established about 1780 by Sewell and Donkin. The ware made at this factory was very pale in colour and though in good style is inferior in potting to that of the best creamware. Enamelled flower painting in the style of Leeds but less vigorous in execution, sometimes occurs on the creamware of this factory (Plate 92A), but most of it was left undecorated. The impressed marks used by this factory are illustrated in Appendix III: 141 to 144. Thomas Fell established the St. Peter's Pottery, Newcastle, in 1817. The principal

[1] See Llewellyn Jewitt, *The Ceramic Art of Great Britain*, London, 1878.

92A SAUCE-TUREEN, pale cream, enamelled in blue, pink and green. Impressed mark 'SEWELL & DONKIN'
ST. ANTHONY'S POTTERY, NEWCASTLE-UPON-TYNE, about 1790, ht. 5⅜ in (14.3 cm)
Victoria and Albert Museum. See page 174

92B DESSERT-BASKET and STAND, pale cream, enamelled in green. Impressed mark 'FELL NEWCASTLE'
ST. PETER'S POTTERY, NEWCASTLE-UPON-TYNE, about 1820, length of stand 10 in (25.5 cm)
Victoria and Albert Museum. See page 176

manufacture was whiteware transfer-printed in black under the glaze. Some pearlware plates with green-feathered borders and decorated in mineral colours with birds or landscapes of which the foliage is frequently 'sponged' in, are sometimes found with the impressed mark 'FELL'. This type of decoration was also done at Liverpool and Bristol. The marks of this factory are illustrated in Appendix III: 145 to 147. A good quality creamware with green enamelling (Plate 92B) is perhaps one of its finest productions.

SUNDERLAND

About the beginning of the nineteenth century a group of potteries situated on the River Wear near Sunderland were producing a whiteware decorated with transfer-prints and pink lustre. This ware can only be regarded as creamware in the very widest sense. The most important of these factories was the Sunderland Pottery, worked by Dixon, Austin, Phillips and Co. from about 1818. Other potteries in this district were the Southwick Pottery founded in 1788 by Anthony Scott, Ford Pottery (South Hylton) founded in 1800 by John Dawson, and the Wear Pottery which was founded by S. Moore and Co. in 1803. Whiteware, transfer-printed in black and washed over in enamel colours with borders of pink lustre, was made by all these. Mugs and jugs of a true creamware, however, are to be found transfer-printed in black and usually coloured over in enamels, with the mark 'Dawson & Co.' in the print. Yellow-glazed creamware and pearlware enamelled in high temperature mineral colours were also produced by this pottery (Plate 93A).

BRISTOL

Joseph Ring took over the delftware pottery at Temple Back from his father-in-law Richard Frank in 1785, for the manufacture of creamware. Knowing nothing of potting himself he engaged Anthony Hassells of Shelton in 1786 to initiate the manufacture and act as manager. Hassells employed workmen from Staffordshire.[1] The creamware was of a whitish body and though well potted was apt to become stained with use. This staining often gives the ware a somewhat dirty appearance, which is further increased by the bluish colour of the glaze. Mugs transfer-printed in umber and coloured over in enamel colours marked 'Bristol Pottery' in the print (Appendix III: 158) were made to celebrate the Treaty of Amiens in 1802 (Plate 93B). A large obelisk in the Fitzwilliam Museum, Cambridge, bears the same print and mark.

A plate in the Victoria and Albert Museum, having an enamel-painted armorial design, is signed 'J. Eaves, Bristol' (Appendix III: 159). Eaves no

[1] See W. J. Pountney, *The Old Bristol Potteries*, London and Bristol, 1920.

93A   PLATE, whiteware, painted in high temperature mineral colours of green, blue and yellow. Inscribed 'Elizh. Kirtley 1829'. Impressed mark 'DAWSON & CO.' FORD POTTERY, SOUTH HYLTON, SUNDERLAND, 1829, diam. 6½ in (16.7 cm) *Victoria and Albert Museum. See page 176*

93B   (i) BARREL, whiteware, painted in high temperature mineral colours of blue, brown and green and inscribed 'Marthar Wilkinson, Bristol Pottery, 1818' BRISTOL, ht. 3⅞ in (9.9 cm)
(ii) MUG, pale cream, transfer-printed in umber and enamelled over in blue, red, yellow, green and brown. Mark in the print 'Bristol Pottery, 1802' BRISTOL, ht. 4⅝ in (11.7 cm)
Victoria and Albert Museum. See pages 176 and 178

doubt enamelled for Joseph Ring. It has often been stated that Ring's creamware was of a chalky white body covered with a bright primrose-coloured or yellow glaze. The creamware referred to is of a very high quality, often painted with sprays of flowers in purplish crimson and sometimes bearing the impressed mark 'HM' (Appendix III:26). This creamware is almost certainly of Leeds origin and not Bristol. The 'HM' mark has no doubt been confused with the mark 'MH' which occurs on ware made at the Bristol Pottery for the Bristol City Council at a later date. The letters 'MH' stand for 'Mansion House'. After 1788 the firm was Ring and Carter and in 1813 John Pountney became a partner, during which period the little barrels with paintings of flowers by William Fifield were made. M. Powell was another painter of the Pountney period. A modified creamware that had a greyish appearance was made by this factory early in the nineteenth century. It was charmingly decorated in underglaze mineral colours of brown, deep blue, sage-green and orange-buff, and was very similar to some ware made at the Leeds Pottery (Plate 93B).

SWANSEA

The Swansea Pottery was founded in 1764 by William Coles. Dated and inscribed pieces make it plain that both saltglaze and creamware were being made here at an early date. A saltglaze flask in The Royal Institute of South Wales is inscribed 'Morgan John Swansea March ye 28th 1768' and an inscribed tea-jar in creamware decorated with coloured glazes is dated 1771; another at the Victoria and Albert Museum is dated 1775. The Swansea creamware at this period can best be described as being interesting but somewhat primitive. During the 1780s creamware decorated with underglaze blue was being produced. This creamware still retained the yellowish glazes of the earlier pieces. William Coles died in 1778 or 1779 leaving the pottery to his three sons and it was then styled John Coles and Company. George Haynes joined the company in 1786 and a certain refinement in the creamware then became apparent and ware showing a strong Wedgwood influence was produced. The firm at this time was Coles and Haynes and from 1801 after the death of Coles it became George Haynes and Company, and from about then or a little before was known as the Cambrian Pottery. Some good plain creamware was then being made as well as pearlware, so much of which was transfer-printed in underglaze-blue and sometimes in a blackish-green or black. Thomas Rothwell the engraver was employed at the Cambrian Pottery for a short time and probably introduced the transfer-printing there.

Much of the enamelling followed the trend of the time, but there was some distinctive painting of natural history subjects. This followed William Dillwyn's purchase of shares in the pottery on his son Lewis Weston Dillwyn's behalf, when the trade name became Haynes, Dillwyn and Company. The

94A   SUGAR-BOWL, pearlware, enamel painted with butterflies in natural colours by
W. W. YOUNG
SWANSEA, about 1805, ht. 5½ in (14 cm)
Victoria and Albert Museum. See page 180
94B   SUPPER-DISH, pearlware, enamel painted in umber by W. W. YOUNG with a
caracal after Thomas Bewick. Inscribed 'caracal' in umber on the back.
SWANSEA, about 1805, length 12 in (30.5 cm)
Towner Collection. See page 180

younger Dillwyn was a naturalist and consequently we find him influencing the enamelling in this direction. Thomas Pardoe who was the pottery's chief enameller from about 1795 executed some good flower, bird and landscape paintings on pearlware known as 'Opaque China', at the Cambrian Pottery. William Weston Young who worked at the pottery from 1803 to 1806 did some admirable copies of butterflies, also birds and animals after Thomas Bewick (Plate 94A and B) and these stand out as the finest contribution to ceramics made by the Cambrian Pottery.

Apart from these, the Swansea wares in the early nineteenth century followed the usual trend of slip-decorated ware in spots, bands and combed decoration, small sprig designs in enamels, high temperature mineral colours and creamware coated with a bright yellow glaze. In 1810 George Haynes retired from the pottery which, with various changes of partnership, continued till 1860 producing many different types of ware, but after Haynes's retirement no further creamware as such was produced. Plates of a heavy whiteware with a ship transfer-printed in a heavy black are to be found with the impressed mark 'DILLWYN & CO.', but the mark used on creamware of the best period, that is to say while George Haynes directed the pottery, was the word 'SWANSEA' impressed.

Chapter 10

CONTINENTAL CREAMWARE

Creamware was not only the principal manufacture in England between the years 1760 and 1820, completely supplanting the manufacture of white saltglaze by about 1780, but it also played a very important part in the history of European ceramics generally. From about 1760, there was an ever increasing export of English creamware to nearly every European country. Eliza Meteyard in her *Life of Josiah Wedgwood* (London, 1865–6) tells us that between 1770 and 1780 Wedgwood had agents in most European countries. By 1783, the Leeds Pottery was exporting vast quantities of creamware to Germany, Holland, France and Spain and other English creamware factories were trading with a number of Continental countries as their pattern books show. Turner of Lane End, the Baddeleys of Shelton and the Warburtons were also exporters on a large scale. In addition potters from Staffordshire, seeing the enormous demand on the Continent for English creamware, left England and set up factories in France. All this activity threatened the very life of the Continental faïence factories and undercut the sale of porcelain as well. In self-defence, they turned from their long established traditions, to the manufacture of creamware; and by the end of the eighteenth century, creamware was being made by every country in Europe. In France creamware was known as *Faïence fine*, or *Faïence anglaise*; in Germany it was *Steingut* and in Sweden *Flintporslin*. Although a number of Continental factories advertised the fact that they deliberately copied the English creamware, in point of fact the Continental and English creamwares often bore little resemblance to each other. Many Continental factories followed their own traditions and developed types of ware in an idiom entirely their own, in order to satisfy their own particular needs or requirements. For example, the use of large tureens, to hold a mixed dish or hot-pot, was much more general in some Continental countries, than in England, consequently countries such as France or Sweden produced large quantities of handsome creamware tureens, which were pieces of importance, often superbly modelled in the rococo manner, and altogether more ambitious than the English counterparts (Plate 96A).

The collector of English creamware may be sometimes puzzled by certain pieces in his collection which are conspicuous by reason of their somewhat different appearance. Such pieces frequently prove to be of Continental origin. The subject of Continental creamware has been very little studied either on the Continent or in England, but a few brief notes on the more important European creamware factories and their wares are subjoined, in the hope that they will be helpful in such cases.

Perhaps the earliest and most important French factory to manufacture a kind of creamware was the PONT-AUX-CHOUX factory at Paris. This was founded in 1743 by Claude Humbert Gérin, who was succeeded in 1747 by Mignon, for the manufacture of *faïence fine* in imitation of English ware. In 1743 creamware in England was only in its infancy but saltglaze was the English ware that was first copied in France. This is borne out by specimens of Pont-aux-Choux manufacture which in colour and general appearance closely resemble English saltglaze,[1] but which, upon closer inspection, would appear to have been glazed with lead. In fact, they have characteristics of both saltglaze and creamware. The creamware made by this factory never seems to have been enamelled, but was decorated with well-moulded floral designs in low relief, which were derived from English saltglaze models. Another type of decoration used extensively by the Pont-aux-Choux factory was the 'barleycorn' pattern, which was a much used pattern on English saltglaze.[2] Amongst the productions of the Pont-aux-Choux factory may be mentioned the large tureens, in the rococo style, the shapes of which were based on silver prototypes. These were magnificent pieces with elaborate covers which were sometimes surmounted by modelled birds, fruit and flowers (Plate 96A). In addition the Pont-aux-Choux factory produced jardinières, jugs, covered mugs and bowls, vases for pot-pourri, sauceboats with or without covers, and figures, some of which depicted Chinese men and women bearing sconces to hold candles. In 1772 the Pont-aux-Choux factory advertised itself as 'Manufacture royale des terres de France à l'imitation de celles d'Angleterre'. These wares, however, are readily distinguishable from the English. The date of the closure of the Pont-aux-Choux factory is not known, but Mignon was still head of the factory in 1786 and it was still working in 1798.

In 1780 two English potters, Charles and Jacob Leigh, who were Roman Catholics, fled to France in order to avoid the violence of the Puritans. In 1781, they founded a factory at DOUAI for the production of 'fayence en grès pâte tendre blanche connue sous le nom de grès d'Angleterre'. The ware was not so thick as that produced by the Pont-aux-Choux factory. At first it was ivory-coloured and of good quality, and was sometimes decorated with pierced open-work designs. Later a whiteware was made which was sometimes painted with

---

[1] Although the ware made at the Pont-aux-Choux factory was generally the whitish colour of English saltglaze, occasionally pieces are found which have a slight tinge of pink.
[2] Saltglaze block-moulds of tableware decorated with the 'barleycorn' pattern are at the Wedgwood Museum, Barlaston, and were used in the manufacture of Wedgwood salt-glazed stoneware.

95   COFFEE-POT, rich cream, enamelled in polychrome colours. Impressed mark
'GM' over 'B'
GIOVANNI MARIA BACCIN, LE NOVE, about 1800, ht. 9¾ in (24.7 cm)
Victoria and Albert Museum. See pages 186 and 187

flowers, religious scenes, masonic emblems or inscriptions in monochrome or polychrome enamel colours. The factory closed in 1831. The ware was mostly unmarked but pieces are sometimes found with 'LEIGH' or 'DOUAI' impressed. Another factory at Douai, which made similar types of ware, was founded in 1799 by Martin Damman. This factory only lasted for eight years.

In 1786 *faïence fine* was being made at CHANTILLY. The ware has a slightly matt appearance and was the colour of English white saltglaze, which it resembled more closely than English creamware. Gilding, especially in lines and in small spotted motifs, seems to have been a favourite form of decoration. Chantilly teapots sometimes have a knob formed of three flowers, as on some porcelain examples from the same factory. The factory mark was a hunting-horn or a fleur-de-lis in colour. In 1792 the factory was sold to Christopher Potter, an Englishman, who manufactured whiteware, the shapes of which were derived from Wedgwood's creamware. This ware was sometimes enamelled in blue or was transfer-printed. Creamware ceased to be made at Chantilly in 1820.

The factory at LUNÉVILLE produced some large well-modelled figures. A bust of Louis XV in a rich butter-coloured creamware is at the Victoria and Albert Museum.

In 1748 Mazois was manufacturing earthenware in imitation of English saltglaze at MONTEREAU. At this date his partner Jean Hill, an Englishman, came to England to discover the process of English saltglaze manufacture. The next year Mazois was making red, black and agate wares, which processes he had learnt in England. In 1756, he had an English partner by the name of Warburton. At this time he was still experimenting with saltglaze. Mazois died in 1774 and the factory was let to an English company directed by William Clark and George or Ralph Shaw.[1] A few years later this firm opened another factory at CREIL. The ware produced by the Montereau and Creil factories from this time was a whiteware which was transfer-printed in black in Paris by Stone, Cocquerel and Le Gros, who added their printed mark. The usual subjects for the engravings of these prints were French or English country houses, and classical, biblical or historic scenes. The ware is often marked 'CREIL' or 'MONTEREAU' impressed (Plate 96B).

After the dissolution of the partnership between Peter and Francis Warburton, Peter became a partner of the New Hall works in Staffordshire, while in 1802 Francis set up a factory at LA CHARITÉ-SUR-LOIRE (Nièvre), for

[1] The name George Shaw is given by the French authorities, Messelet and Haumont. George may have been the son of Ralph Shaw and possibly succeeded his father as director (or manager) of the firm. Solon, *French Faïence*, gives Ralph Shaw of Burslem, manager with W. Clark of Newcastle-under-Lyme. Ralph Shaw of Burslem left for Paris in 1736 as a result of his losing a law case which he brought against another potter for the infringement of a patent (see Josiah C. Wedgwood, *Staffordshire Pottery and its History*, London, 1914, p. 58). Ralph Shaw whilst at Burslem made slipware and sgraffito ware on which patterns were made by cutting away the slip to reveal the contrasting colour of the body underneath. Simeon Shaw in his *History of the Staffordshire Potteries*, Hanley, 1829, states that Ralph Shaw glazed his ware with salt. If this was the case, a form of saltglaze may have been introduced into France soon after 1736.

96A TUREEN, cream
     PONT-AUX-CHOUX, PARIS, about 1770, ht. 10 in (25.5 cm), width 12¾ in (32.5
     cm)
     Towner Collection. See pages 180 and 182

96B CUP and SAUCER, whiteware, transfer-printed in black by STONE, COCQUEREL
     AND LE GROS of Paris. Impressed 'CREIL'
     CREIL, about 1785, ht. of cup 2½ in (6.4 cm), diam. of saucer 4⅞ in (12.1 cm)
     Victoria and Albert Museum. See page 184

the manufacture of whiteware, some of which was marked 'LA CHARITÉ' impressed. Landscapes painted in black and dark brown are found on the creamware of the BELLEVUE factory near Toul, and a yellowish creamware was made at APT. In general the French creamware was heavier and less refined than the English. The glazes also differed from those used in this country both in quality and colour.

The chief creamware factory in Belgium was at ANDENNE, where a factory was founded in 1784 by Joseph Wouters. The ware produced was white decorated with enamel painting or transfer-printing in blue. The factory mark was 'ADW' impressed.

In Germany the factory at DURLACH produced creamware some of which was decorated with vine-leaf borders either painted in black or brown, or moulded in relief. The factory mark was 'DURLACH' impressed. The creamware made at HUBERTUSBERG at the end of the eighteenth century was sometimes marked 'WEDGWOOD' impressed. At KÖNIGSBERG (East Prussia), Johann Ehrenreich made creamware from about 1780. Relief borders in rococo taste picked out in blue are typical of the decoration used by this factory. The mark was the letter 'K' impressed.

Between 1786 and 1827 the HOLITSCH factory in Hungary made a medium-quality creamware which was either decorated with pierced open-work borders or enamelled with conventional patterns. The mark was the name 'HOLITSCH' or the letter 'H' impressed. Some black transfer-printing on a coarse whiteware was done at LUXEMBOURG.

Creamware was made at MARIEBERG in Sweden at least as early as 1770, when regular production started. By this date the factory was being run by Henrik Sten, and the factory mark was 'MB STEN', incised. In 1782 Marieberg was sold to the Rörstrand factory, and was finally closed in 1788. The RÖRSTRAND factory, which continues to the present day, probably began the manufacture of creamware in 1771. Much of it showed a strong English influence, and in particular there was a close affinity to Wedgwood. A smaller factory at GUSTAFSBERG-VÄNGE, not far from Upsala (not to be confused with the still-surviving manufacture at Gustafsberg on Värmdö, founded in 1827) made simple creamware after Sten's arrival there in 1786. Later small Swedish factories included LÖFNÄS, near Mariefred, run from about 1800 by P. A. Schirmer, Sten's successor at Marieberg; and ULFSUNDA, near Stockholm, directed by the modeller C. A. Linning.

In Denmark an existing company for the manufacture of faience at RENDSBORG in Schleswig-Holstein was reformed in 1772 to make creamware under the technical leadership of C. F. G. Clar, but failed about 1818. It used as a mark 'R' or 'RF' impressed. The faience factory at KASTRUP, near Copenhagen, similarly took up creamware manufacture about 1772, coming under the guidance of J. C. L. Mantzius, who left Rendsborg some time before 1781. The Kastrup mark was 'CW' (perhaps for 'Castrup Waerk') over 'M' (for 'Mantzius'), impressed. At RØNNE, on the clay-rich island of Bornholm, an

Englishman, James Davenport, manufactured creamware from 1792, but the factory closed in 1800 after he left for America. A second manufacture under the manager Johann Spietz made creamware there until his death in 1834, and continued thereafter under his sons. The factory mark was an impressed 'B' within an irregular circle, above the name 'SPIETZ' or the initials 'JS', incised. The GUDUMLUND factory was worked between 1804 and 1814 by Count Schimmelmann. A bee impressed was used as a mark on the creamware of this factory between 1808 and 1820, when the factory was closed. The Danish creamwares were often of high quality, and apart from straight copies of the English wares, pottery with moulded and openwork decoration was common, sometimes painted in high-temperature blue or manganese-purple, while Rendsborg was notable for its ambitious figural centrepieces. Wedgwood's marbled wares with relief ornaments in cream were also copied, while Clar at Rendsborg even imitated his unglazed stoneware.

Very little is known of the creamware that was made in Italy, but several examples which were made at NAPLES are exhibited at the Victoria and Albert Museum as well as a fine coffee-pot from LE NOVE (Plate 95). The two main factories at Naples were conducted by the Vecchio family and the Giustiniani family. The ware made at the former factory is nearly white in colour and is of fine quality. The decorations for the most part consist of elaborate enamel painting, which is more pictorial than decorative. The factory mark is 'F.D.V.N.' standing for F. del Vecchio, Napoli. The ware made by the Giustiniani family at Naples about 1815 is of a rich cream colour, decorated with pierced open-work. This ware is thicker than the Leeds creamware, though nearly resembling it in other respects. Such ware is sometimes marked 'BG' impressed, standing for Biagio Giustiniani. The Le Nove coffee-pot closely approaches the quality of the finest English creamware though differing in shape, detail and decoration. The Victoria and Albert Museum specimen has plain double intertwined handles without terminals. The pot is skilfully enamelled with a scene inspired by the paintings of Watteau (Plate 95). This coffee-pot is marked with the letters 'G.M' impressed, which stand for Giovanni Maria Baccin. A star in red enamel also occurs as a mark of this factory. Mention must be made of an interesting potter and decorator of SAVONA, named Giacomo Boselli, alias Jacques Boselly. His enamelling is usually in brick red or brown. Specimens of creamware made by the Leeds and Wedgwood factories were also enamelled and signed by him. His signature, which is usually painted in brown, consists of the name 'Giacomo Boselli' or the French form 'Jacques Boselly'. A plate at the Victoria and Albert Museum which is transfer-printed in red, is signed 'Jacques Bosselly'.

In Spain during the early nineteenth century, creamware was manufactured at ALCORA. Some beautifully modelled figure groups, of a rich cream-colour, were amongst the productions of this factory.

Appendix I

HANDLES, SPOUTS, KNOBS, TERMINALS AND BORDERS

Much help in identifying the origin of creamware may be gained by a comparison of some of the moulded details. From a close study of the pattern books and marked specimens it has been discovered that there exists a remarkable consistency of design and character in the moulded details of individual creamware factories which will be found to differ to a very great extent from those of other factories. This fact, which is most remarkable, becomes more and more apparent as one studies the wares and must indicate that each pottery employed its own modellers for the enormous amount of continuous moulded work necessary for the factory's output. There are instances however when more than one factory uses the same small moulded design. In most cases these would seem to be copies, as slight differences between them are often discernible; others may be the work of outside modellers who sold their work to various factories, but it is not likely that such outside modellers would supply such small moulds as those in question but rather the more important ones such as figures, jugs, teapots etc., but even here it is evident that factories made their own copies in many cases. Perhaps the most notable overlapping of these small moulded patterns occurs between the Leeds and Melbourne potteries suggesting that a modeller moved from one to the other factory taking some of his moulds with him or in some way supplied both factories. One of the surprises is that the two largest creamware factories—Wedgwood and Leeds—hardly varied their small moulded designs at all during the last quarter of the eighteenth century. This may have been in order to conform to their printed pattern books. The Cockpit Hill factory on the other hand, though never varying their teapot spout or plain double handle, produced an enormous number of different handle and flower knob terminals during this period, yet all in character with one another and clearly the work of one modeller, and none of which are to be found on the wares of any other factory.

In this study it has been possible to illustrate only a very few of the enormous variety of moulded details on creamware. Those selected are chosen because they are particularly characteristic and give a clear indication of the factory where they were produced. When a particular design is known to have been used by more than one factory, this, of course, has been stated. It should be emphasized however that a single detail, while often of attributive value, normally requires further corroborative evidence to give weight to an attribution.

PLATE I : SPOUTS

Plate I, fig. 1

The crabstock spout (Plates 7A and 42B) accompanied by a similar handle (Plate IV: 1), was first introduced on saltglaze teapots and punch-pots about 1745, though it had earlier prototypes. It is found also on unglazed redware, glazed blackware and colour-glazed ware of the 'Whieldon' type, and was naturally adopted as the earliest form of spout on creamware made in Staffordshire, Liverpool, Yorkshire and Derbyshire. Although the handle on the cover of saltglaze teapots was often of crabstock form, except for a very few examples, this was replaced on creamware teapots by a ball, mushroom, or flower-shaped knob. Crabstock spouts and handles ceased to be made about 1770.

Plate I, fig. 2

Hexagonal or faceted spout, with small moulded ornamentations, about 1763–77 (Plates 38B and 40A, B). This spout was normally accompanied by the faceted loop handle (Plate IV: 5) but it frequently occurs with other types of handle, particularly the scroll handle (Plate IV: 3B). It was probably first modelled by W. Greatbatch for Whieldon and Wedgwood, but was much more extensively made at Cockpit Hill, Derby.

Plate I, fig. 3

Plain hexagonal or faceted spout, about 1763–77 (Plates 38A and 39A). Although this spout was used extensively on saltglaze, as far as is known the only creamware examples of it are of Cockpit Hill, Derby, origin.

Plate I, fig. 4

Rococo spout, about 1760–85 (Plate 58A). There were several variations of this spout of which that on Plate III: 2 is another example. They seem to occur on both Leeds and Cockpit Hill creamware. A transfer-printed teapot in the Leeds City Art Galleries having this spout is signed 'Leeds Pottery' in the print.

Plate I, fig. 5

Fern pattern, about 1760–70 (Plate 59A). Some known examples of this spout would appear to be of Leeds origin, but it may have originated in Staffordshire. It was often used in conjunction with the handle, Plate V: 4.

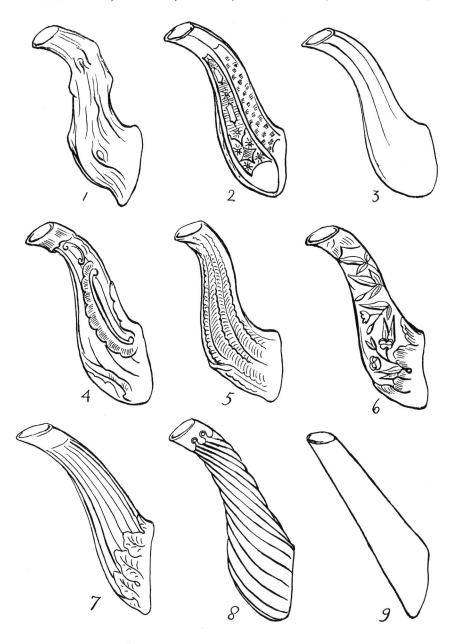

I Creamware Spouts. *See pages 190, 192*

Plate I, fig. 6
Floral pattern, about 1765–75 (Plate 39B). This pattern was probably only used at Cockpit Hill, Derby, and was usually accompanied by the handle, Plate IV: 3b.

Plate I, fig. 7
Fluted spout with leaves at the base, about 1760–80. This type of spout seems to have been in general manufacture. Examples from Staffordshire and Leeds are known.

Plate I, fig. 8
Twisted spout, about 1760–70. This was one of the earliest types of Leeds spout. It was often used in conjunction with the twisted handle, Plate V: 5, but was used elsewhere as well.

Plate I, fig. 9
Straight spout, about 1770 (Plate 50A). This type of creamware spout was made at Melbourne and probably elsewhere. It was also made in unglazed redware and black basalt ware by a number of factories.

PLATE II: SPOUTS (continued)

Plate II, fig. 1
Cabbage or cauliflower spout, about 1760–80 (Plate 9A). This spout, which was used very extensively by Wedgwood, was probably modelled in the first place by William Greatbatch for Wedgwood's cauliflower ware. It was copied by a number of other factories. Wedgwood examples on creamware are always accompanied by one of the following handles, Plate IV: 3, 3A, Plate V: 1, 2, 3.

Plate II, fig. 2
Shell spout, about 1764–85. This spout was modelled in 1764 by William Greatbatch for Wedgwood, who used it for both teapots and coffee-pots (Plate 25), and was used by him in conjunction with the handle, Plate V: 3.

Plate II, fig. 3
Simple shell spout, about 1764–85 (Plate 16B). This spout may have been modelled by William Greatbatch for Wedgwood or Whieldon. A spout of this pattern was excavated at Fenton Low, and is now at the Castle Museum, Norwich. It is likely to have been copied by other factories.

Plate II, fig. 4
Spout with enfolding acanthus at base, about 1775–80. This spout occurs on Leeds pottery and is usually accompanied by the handle Plate V: 8, and knob Plate VII: 4. It was also used by the Melbourne Pottery in combination with the handle Plate VI: 2 and knob Plate VIII: 2 (Plate 56B).

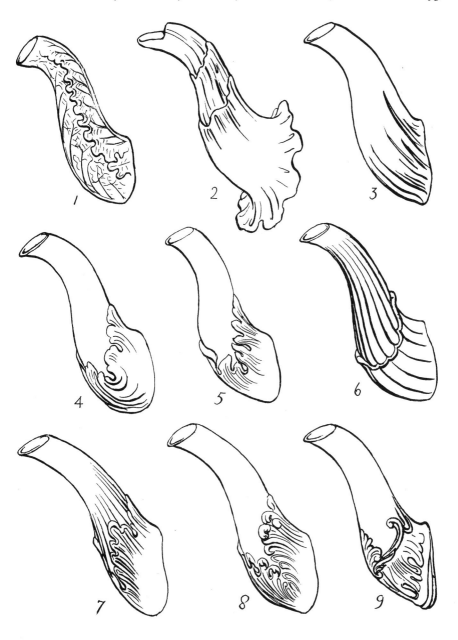

II Creamware Spouts. *See pages 192, 194*

Plate II, fig. 5
Spout with acanthus at base, about 1770–1815 (Plate 65A). This spout was very extensively used by the Leeds Pottery. It is shown in the pattern books and specimens marked 'LEEDS * POTTERY' are known; it does not appear to have been used on any other eighteenth-century creamware. It is usually accompanied by the handle Plate V:8, and knob Plate VII:4.

Plate II, fig. 6
Fluted spout springing from a fluted base, about 1775–85 (Plate 66B). This type of spout appears to have been made at the Leeds Pottery only.

Plate II, figs 7, 8 and 9
About 1775–85 (Plates 35 and 36). These three spouts were used in conjunction with the indented curve or ear-shaped handle Plate IV:6, and either the flower knob Plate VII:1, or a pierced ball knob. Teapots with these characteristics are often decorated with black transfer-prints coloured over with enamel, some of which are signed by William Greatbatch. The spout Plate II:9 only seems to occur on the coloured transfer-printed teapots, and is probably Staffordshire. Shards of Plate II:7 were found on the site of the William Bacchus pottery at Little Fenton and Plate II:8 on the Greatbatch site.

PLATE III: SPOUTS (continued)

Plate III, fig. 1
This spout, sometimes known as the 'wrapped leaf' spout, was used by Wedgwood on some of his fruit teapots for which it was probably designed, but it was also used for some of his early transfer-printed creamware such as the Masonic teapot in the British Museum (Plate 11B). It was clearly designed to be used in conjunction with the handle shown on Plate IV:3.

Plate III, fig. 2
There are several variations of this spout (see Plate I:4). This particular pattern seems to have been used by both the Leeds and Cockpit Hill factories and it is possible that it was used by others (Plate 46A).

Plate III, fig. 3
This spout which is of a basket-work pattern with a strawberry motive towards the base denotes a Cockpit Hill origin. It has not so far been discovered on the wares of any other factory (Plate 46B).

Plate III, fig. 4
This is the spout most frequently found on teapots made at the Derbyshire factory of Melbourne (Plates 53A, 55A and 56A). It does not appear to have been made elsewhere.

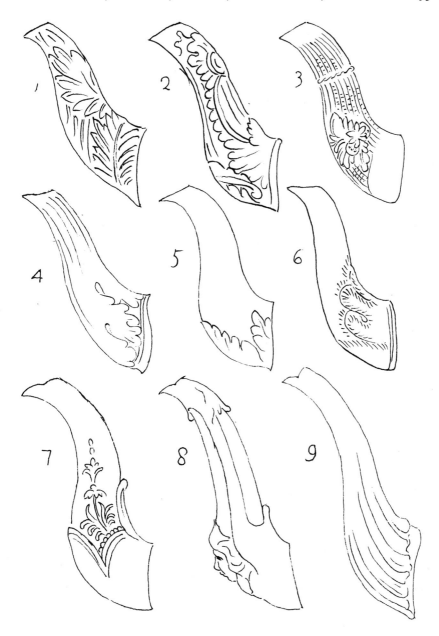

III Creamware Spouts. *See pages 194, 196*

Plate III, fig. 5
This is a spout which denotes a Cockpit Hill origin and has not been found on the ware of any other factory. It is usually accompanied by the double handle shown on Plate VI:8 but with various terminals such as those on Plate X:1, 2 and 3 (Plate 44A and B).

Plate III, fig. 6
Shards of this spout were excavated on the site of the Melbourne Pottery, but teapots with this identical spout are rare though some, which for other reasons are clearly of Melbourne origin, have spouts which closely resemble it. The Leeds Pottery seems to have made a spout very similar in character but not identical with it.

Plate III, figs. 7, 8 and 9
These are three spouts used by the Leeds Pottery. A block-mould for fig. 7 was excavated on the site of the Leeds Pottery. It is illustrated on Plate 44 of *English Cream-coloured Earthenware* and occurs on a transfer-printed coffee-pot in the Yorkshire Museum with a design of a bullfight marked 'Leeds Pottery' in the print. Fig. 8 was commonly used by the Leeds Pottery for punch-kettles (Plates 68 and 79B). Fig. 9 was not only used by the Leeds Pottery for coffee-pots but also by the 'w.B.' factory at Little Fenton (see page 84) where shards of a teapot spout of this pattern were excavated.

PLATE IV: HANDLES

Plate IV, fig. 1
Crabstock, about 1745–70 (Plate 7A). This handle was usually accompanied by the crabstock spout and was of general manufacture (see notes on the crabstock spout, Plate I:1).

Plate IV, fig. 2
Flat-loop or strap handle, about 1745–70. This handle was used for coffee-pots, chocolate-pots, jugs and mugs, but never seems to have been used for teapots. It is the earliest form of handle to be found on creamware of these descriptions. It originated in saltglaze about 1740 and was also used for unglazed redware, glazed blackware and solid agate ware. Although it is often associated with the work of Thomas Whieldon, it was used by other potters as well, and there are known examples of Yorkshire, Liverpool, and Derby origin besides those of Staffordshire. Plate IV:2a is a variation of the pinched end.

Plate IV, fig. 3
Scroll handle, about 1760–70. There were a number of variations of the scroll handle, of which four of the most usual types are illustrated (Plate IV:3, 3a, b, c). The earliest of these, fig. 3, was used by Wedgwood for his first transfer-

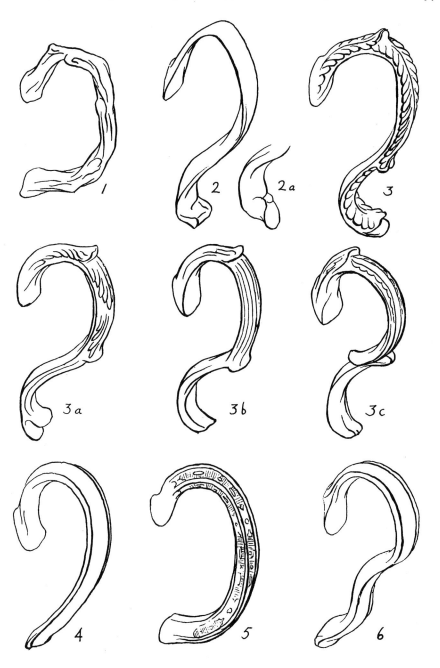

IV Creamware Handles. *See pages 196, 198, 199*

printed creamware of 1761 (Plate 10). It was, however, quickly copied by other factories. The Wedgwood examples are usually sharper in modelling than the copies. It is also to be found on ware with mottled glazes of Wedgwood origin. It was used for teapots and coffee-pots and was usually accompanied by the cauliflower spout and pierced ball or mushroom knob on Wedgwood creamware.

Plate IV, fig. 3a
Scroll handle, about 1765–75. This variation of the scroll handle was first used by Wedgwood for creamware a few years later than the previous one, and is to be found on early Wedgwood teapots made before about 1775, where it is usually accompanied by the cauliflower spout (Plate II: 1) and pierced ball knob (Plate VIII: 3). It was also used by Wedgwood for his cauliflower teapots. Though this variety of the scroll handle may have been used by other Staffordshire potters who were closely associated with Wedgwood, it is essentially a Wedgwood handle (Plate 15B).

Plate IV, fig. 3b
Scroll handle, about 1765–75. This variety of the scroll handle is in close imitation of the Wedgwood one (Plate IV: 3a), and was used a great deal by the Cockpit Hill factory, Derby (Plate 38B), usually accompanied by spouts Plate I: 2, 3 or 6, and a small pierced knob like a button (Plate VIII: 16).

Plate IV, fig. 3c
Scroll handle, about 1765–75. This variety of the scroll handle occurs on the creamware of the Cockpit Hill, Derby factory (Plate 40B) where it was used in conjunction with the spout Plate I: 2, and on some teapots with mottled glazes. Some teapots with this handle may be of Staffordshire origin.

Plate IV, fig. 4
Simple loop, from about 1760 (Plate 16B). This handle was first introduced by Wedgwood for his green-glazed creamware on which it was accompanied by the shell spout (see note for Plate II: 3). Although variations of it have been made by most factories ever since, it seems to have been discarded by Wedgwood, in this particular form, by about 1770.

Plate IV, fig. 5
Faceted loop, about 1763–70. This handle which was usually accompanied by the faceted spout (Plate I: 2 and 3) was probably first modelled by William Greatbatch for Whieldon and Wedgwood. It was extensively used at Cockpit Hill, Derby, where in some instances the small moulded patterns on it were omitted (Plate 39A). Examples also occur on ware decorated with coloured glazes.

Plate IV, fig. 6
Indented loop, about 1770–85. The manufacture of handles of this shape was
very general (Plates 35A, B, 36A and 80A).

PLATE V: HANDLES (continued)

Plate V, fig. 1
Loop with overlapping scales, about 1770–90 (Plate 18B). This was the handle
most generally adopted by Wedgwood for teapots and jugs of the Etruria
period. It does not appear to have been made by any other factory. It was used
in conjunction with the cauliflower spout (Plate II:1).

Plate V, fig. 2
Plain loop with curled base, about 1770–90 (Plate 16A). This handle denotes a
Wedgwood origin, but is much more rare than the double variety (see Plate
V:3). It was used for teapots and jugs. On teapots it was accompanied by the
cauliflower spout (Plate II:1) and pierced ball knob (Plate VIII:3).

Plate V, fig. 3
Double intertwined handle with curled extremities, about 1775–90. This
handle was used by Wedgwood for teapots, coffee-pots and jugs. He also used a
very similar handle for cups. It was copied and made to a limited extent at
Castleford. The Wedgwood handle of this type was usually accompanied by the
cauliflower spout (Plate II:1), though it is sometimes found in conjunction with
the shell spout (Plate II:2) (Plate 25).

Plate V, fig. 4
Double intertwined handle, joined at the base, about 1770 (Plate 59A). This
handle was made at the Leeds Pottery for teapots and was usually accompanied
by the fern spout (Plate I:5). It may also have been produced in Staffordshire.

Plate V, fig. 5
Double intertwined and twisted handle, the ends covered by terminals, about
1770 (Plate 58A). This was a type of handle made at the Leeds and Melbourne
Potteries.

Plate V, fig. 6
Reeded loop with foliate base, about 1770 (Plate 19). This is a Wedgwood
pattern, the mould for which, dated 1768, is in the Wedgwood Museum,
Barlaston. It is not known to have been made by any other factory, though
there are others somewhat like it of different manufactures. It is sometimes
accompanied by the spout Plate I:7.

Plate V, fig. 7
Double intertwined handle with foliate ends, about 1770. This occurs on teapots of uncertain origin. It is sometimes associated with a straight spout (Plate I:9), which points to a Melbourne origin.

Plate V, fig. 8
Reeded double intertwined handle with terminals, about 1775–1815 (Colour Plate G). This handle was used very extensively at Leeds for teapots, coffee-pots, jugs, mugs, etc. It is shown in the Leeds drawing books and pattern books. The usual terminals used for this handle are Plate IX:5, 11 and 13. It is usually accompanied by spouts Plate II:4, 5, 6, and flower knobs Plate VII:4, 4a, b, c. This handle when used in conjunction with the terminals enumerated above, does not appear to have been made by any other factory. It should be noted that the Leeds handles are more finely and evenly reeded than those of most other factories, the number of reeds being seldom less than five and sometimes as many as eleven.

Plate V, fig. 9
Double intertwined handle with foliate ends, about 1780–1820 (Plate 78). This handle and another which has foliate ends of a slightly different pattern seem to be peculiar to the Leeds Pottery and were used extensively on the later creamware. They are both illustrated in the Leeds pattern book, but a closely similar handle is illustrated in the Castleford pattern book.

PLATE VI: HANDLES (continued)

Plate VI, fig. 1
This is the later form of double handle made by the Melbourne Pottery in Derbyshire (Plate 55A and B). It was also used with other terminals such as Plate IX:12 and was usually associated with the spout Plate III:4.

Plate VI, fig. 2
This is another Melbourne handle also used in conjunction with the spout Plate III:4 (Plate 56A and B).

Plate VI, fig. 3
This handle is somewhat rare and was used for small jugs of Leeds or Staffordshire origin.

Plate VI, fig. 4
This is the faceted Cockpit Hill teapot handle which usually went with the spout shown on Plate I:3 (Plate 39A).

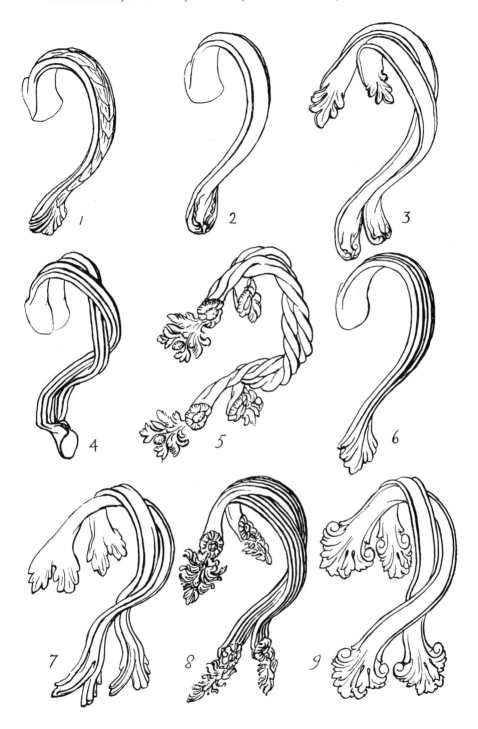

V Creamware Handles. *See pages 199–200*

Plate VI, fig. 5
This handle was drawn from a teapot impressed 'WEDGWOOD & CO.' and therefore made at Ferrybridge.

Plate VI, figs. 6 and 6a
Shards of this handle which has quite a sharp spine were excavated on the site of the Melbourne Pottery in Derbyshire. So far no teapot with this handle has yet been found though a coffee-pot in the Leeds City Art Galleries possesses it in a double form. Fig. 6a shows the section through it.

Plate VI, figs. 7 and 7a
This drawing was taken from a teapot of uncertain origin. Shards of this handle, without terminals, were found on the site of the Melbourne Pottery. Fig. 7a shows the section of it. It occurs on the Melbourne teapot (Plate 50A) but with the terminal Plate X: 12.

Plate VI, fig. 8
This double handle was drawn from a transfer-printed teapot made by the Cockpit Hill factory at Derby. Though many different patterns of terminal were used in conjunction with this handle (see Plate X: 1, 2 and 3) yet the handle itself was invariably plain without any form of fluting or reeding.

Plate VI, fig. 9
This handle was used for a Melbourne puzzle-jug, now at Colonial Williamsberg.

PLATE VII: KNOBS

Plate VII, figs. 1, 1a and 1b
Convolvulus with frilled edge, about 1770–85. The same flower knob is shown on each of these three drawings, but the terminals differ. A drawing of a covered jug in one of the Leeds drawing books has a knob which is no doubt intended to represent fig. 1a. Fig. 1b occurs on some Leeds creamware made before 1775. Fig. 1 occurs on enamelled creamware believed to be Leeds (Plates 80A and B) as well as on teapots with engravings by William Greatbatch (Plates 35B and 36). A Staffordshire origin for these knobs is therefore also indicated. Fig. 1 is usually accompanied by the handle Plate IV:6, and the spouts Plate II:7, 8 and 9 (see under these for additional notes).

Plate VII, figs. 2 and 2a
Convolvulus, about 1770 (Colour Plate F). These show the same flower but in fig. 2a the edge has been cut by hand to form petals. They seem to have been used by the Leeds Pottery before 1775. Some very similar knobs were made by the Pont-aux-Choux factory in Paris (see page 182).

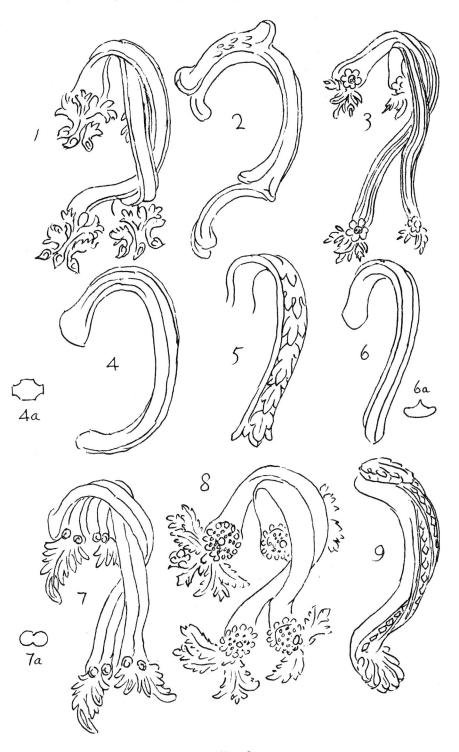

VI Creamware Handles. *See pages 200, 202*

Plate VII, figs. 3 and 3a

Convolvulus with straight markings, about 1770 (Plate 58A and B). This flower knob is one of the first to have been made at the Leeds Pottery. The accompanying applied terminal varies considerably.

Plate VII, figs. 4, 4a, 4b and 4c

Flower with terminal of two buds, about 1770–1820 (Plate 65A). This is the usual flower knob found on Leeds teapots made after 1775, though it occasionally occurs on the earlier deep cream Leeds teapots as well (Plate 59A). It is the type of flower knob usually depicted in the Leeds pattern books, and it is usually accompanied by the handle Plate V:8, and one of the spouts Plate II:4, 5 and 6 (see under these for additional notes). The flower is made in two parts, a flat button-like form being superimposed upon a conical one with a nick at the base. This construction seems to be peculiar to the Leeds Pottery. The flower, fig. 4c, was used to decorate the figure group in the Victoria and Albert Museum (Plate 75).

Plate VII, fig. 5

Reflex flower with spiral centre, about 1775–85. This flower occurs on coffee-pots of Leeds manufacture both in plain or enamelled creamware and on tortoiseshell ware (Plate 82). It was also sometimes used by the Wedgwood factory in the nineteenth and twentieth centuries for tea-ware and covered open-work cake-baskets. The usual eighteenth-century Wedgwood knob for these is shown on Plate VII:8.

Plate VII, fig. 6

Convolvulus with terminal of three leaves, about 1765–80 (Plates 52, 53A, B and 55A). This type of convolvulus when it is combined with the three leaves shown seems to be peculiar to the Melbourne Pottery, which used it a great deal.

Plate VII, fig. 7

The spiral centre, about 1780–1820. This flower knob differs from the preceding knobs with spiral centres in that each one was made separately; the petals were attached by hand and a spiral coil applied to the centre. It was mostly used for covered bowls. A large covered cream-bowl in the Fitzwilliam Museum, Cambridge with this knob and another in the author's collection are both impressed 'W (***)' which mark is ascribed to Enoch Wood (Plate 32). This knob was also used by the Staffordshire firm of Whitehead.

Plate VII, fig. 8

A Wedgwood flower knob, about 1770–1820 (Plate 25). This flower knob was used very extensively by Wedgwood. It does not appear to have been made by any other factory. On teapots it was usually accompanied by the spouts Plate II:1 and 2, and the handle Plate V:3.

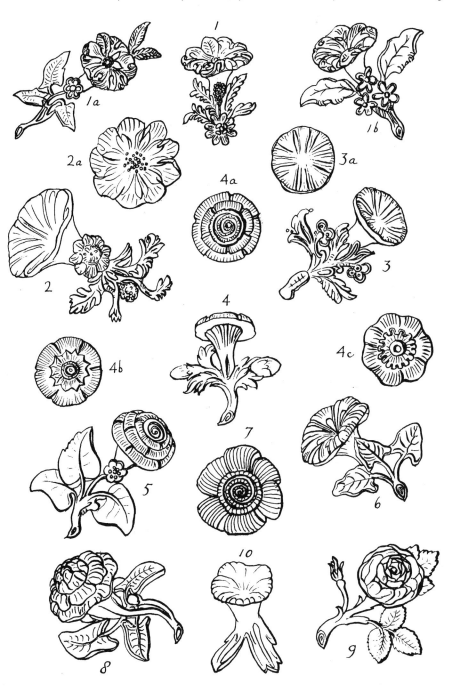

VII Creamware Knobs. *See pages 202, 204, 206*

Plate VII, fig. 9
Rose, about 1775–1800 (Plate 26B). This is a Wedgwood knob. It does not appear to have been used to the same extent as the previous one, nor does it appear to have been made by any other factory. It was mostly used for smaller pots such as small covered jugs and butter-dishes.

Plate VII, fig. 10
Convolvulus without applied terminals, about 1770. This flower knob is of uncertain origin. It is sometimes accompanied by the handle Plate V:7, and the straight spout Plate I:9, and may therefore be of Melbourne origin.

PLATE VIII: KNOBS (continued)

Plate VIII, figs. 1, 4 and 7
Shards of these teapot knobs were excavated on the site of the Melbourne Pottery in Derbyshire, which is believed to have been the only pottery to pierce the flower knobs on the teapot covers for a steam-vent.

Plate VIII, fig. 2
So far as is known this fluted form of acorn knob was only used by the Melbourne Pottery (Plate 56B).

Plate VIII, fig. 3
This was the usual type of Wedgwood teapot knob (Plate 10, etc.).

Plate VIII, figs. 5, 8, 13 and 15
Shards of these knobs were excavated on the site of the Whieldon works at Little Fenton (sometimes called Fenton Vivian). The bird knob (fig. 13) was however undoubtedly used by a number of other potteries as well.

Plate VIII, figs. 6 and 11
These were early forms of knob used by the Leeds Pottery.

Plate VIII, fig. 10
This is one of the forms of convolvulus flower knob used by the Cockpit Hill factory at Derby. It was almost invariably painted with a red band round the outer edge and was accompanied by the spout Plate III:5, and either the handle Plate VI:8 with various terminals such as those on Plate X:1, 2 and 3, or the handle shown on Plate IV:6 (Plate 44A and B).

Plate VIII, fig. 12
This was a type of Melbourne flower knob, pierced through the centre to form a steam-vent as in Plate VIII:4. No other factory seems to have done this.

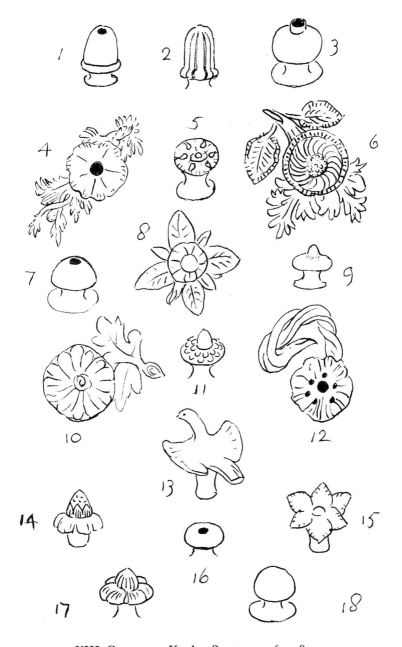

VIII Creamware Knobs. *See pages 206, 208*

Plate VIII, fig. 14
This knob, of which there were several slight variations, was used by the Cockpit Hill factory at Derby (Plate 40A).

Plate VIII, fig. 16
This very distinctive knob which is very flattened in form and pierced, is particularly indicative of the Cockpit Hill factory at Derby (Plates 38A, 39A and B).

Plate VIII, fig. 17
This knob was used in Staffordshire, Yorkshire and Derbyshire.

Plate VIII, fig. 18
This simple global knob was used by the Melbourne Pottery, the Leeds Pottery and at Liverpool (Plate 90A).

PLATE IX: TERMINALS

A great number of different terminals were used on creamware to cover the join of handles and knobs to the pot. The terminals illustrated on Plates IX and X are those of most usual occurrence.

Plate IX, figs. 1, 2, 3, 6, 7 and 8
This type of terminal in which a berry between leaves is conspicuous, is found on the deep cream-coloured ware made before 1775. Plate X:4, 7 and 8 show three more. It was used on teapots, coffee-jugs, tureens etc. Plate IX:3 is from a fragment taken from the site of the Fenton Low works and is the terminal to a double handle. Fig. 6 is a Melbourne version, of which others are shown on Plate X. Figs. 1, 2, 7 and 8 are probably all Leeds or made in the Leeds district.

Plate IX, fig. 4
This seems to occur on both Leeds and Melbourne creamware.

Plate IX, fig. 5
This occurs on Leeds creamware of both the deep and pale colours. It is not known on the ware of any other factory (Plate 57B).

Plate IX, figs. 9, 10, 14 and 15
These small terminals occur on small pieces of Leeds creamware and are illustrated in the Leeds pattern and drawing books.

Plate IX, fig. 11
This terminal was used very extensively by the Leeds Pottery from about 1775–1820 (Plate 67 etc.). It is frequently shown in the pattern book and occurs on marked pieces. It is not known on the ware of any other factory.

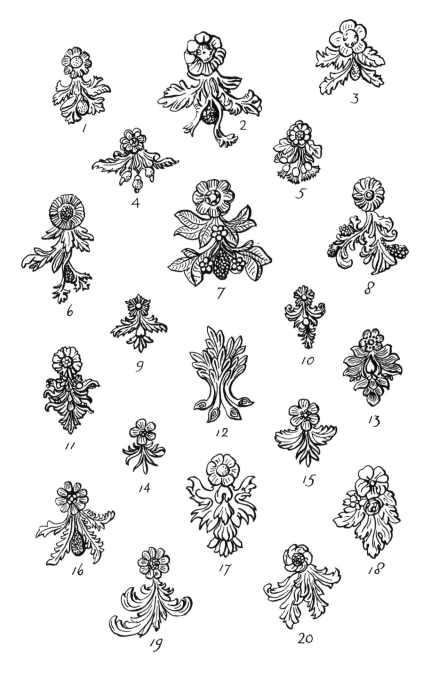

IX Creamware Terminals. *See pages 208, 210*

Plate IX, fig. 12
This terminal was used by the Melbourne Pottery in conjunction with the flower knob Plate VII:6, and spout Plate III:4. It is not known on the ware of any other factory.

Plate IX, fig. 13
This terminal occurs on Leeds creamware, about 1770–90. It is not known on the ware of any other factory.

Plate IX, fig. 16
This terminal occurs on teapots bearing prints engraved by William Great-batch and coloured over in enamels (Plates 35 and 36). (See under Plate II:7, 8 and 9.) A Staffordshire origin for such pieces is indicated. It was mostly used in conjunction with the flower knob, Plate VII:1. It also occurs on pieces of probable Leeds origin.

Plate IX, fig. 17
This terminal is of uncertain origin, but was perhaps made at Leeds or Liverpool or by Shorthose, about 1775–80.

Plate IX, fig. 18
This terminal occurs on Leeds creamware in conjunction with the flower knob Plate VII:5, about 1775–85.

Plate IX, fig. 19
This terminal occurs on some creamware made before 1775, but its origin is uncertain.

Plate IX, fig. 20
This terminal occurs on very fine quality creamware enamelled by D. Rhodes, and is probably of Leeds origin.

PLATE X: TERMINALS (continued)

Plate X, figs. 1, 2, 3 and 5
These are terminals used by the Cockpit Hill factory at Derby. These are only a few of the many different designs for handle terminals used by this factory. 1, 2 and 3 were used in conjunction with the spout on Plate III:5 and the knob Plate VIII:10, which last was almost invariably decorated with a red enamelled outside edge. Fig. 5a shows the section through the Cockpit Hill double handle which was always plain. Another design of Cockpit Hill terminal is shown on Plate VI:8 (Plate 44 A and B).

Plate X, figs. 4, 6, 7, 8, 9 and 12
These are types of handle terminal used by the Melbourne factory in

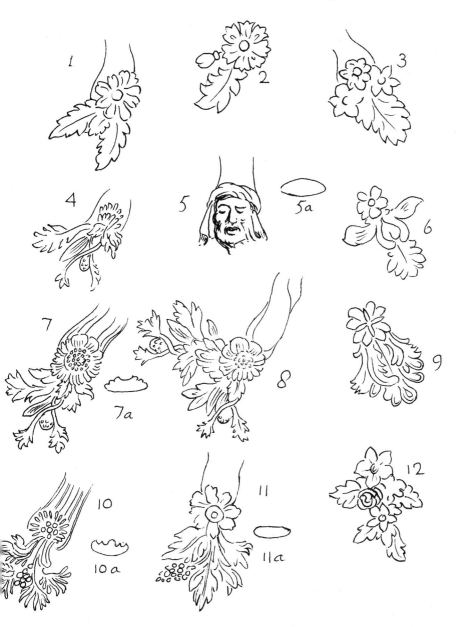

X Creamware Terminals. *See pages 210, 212*

Derbyshire. Figs. 4, 7 and 9 are from shards found on the factory site. A further Melbourne handle terminal is shown on Plate VI:1 which is usually used in conjunction with the spout shown on Plate III:4 and the flower knob on Plate VII:6. Fig. 7a shows the section through the Melbourne reeded double handle (Plate 52).

Plate X, figs. 10 and 10a
These show what is believed to be the usual handle terminal used by the Rothwell Pottery in Yorkshire. This belief is based on pieces having the same very distinctive mottled decoration as pieces found on the site of the Rothwell Pottery. Fig. 10a shows the section through the reeded handle (Plate 87).

Plate X, figs. 11 and 11a
These are drawn from shards excavated on the site of a pottery at Little Fenton. A number of pieces found on this site are impressed with the letters 'WB' in monogram. This mark is attributed to William Bacchus. No complete specimen has yet been found bearing this terminal.

PLATE XI: MOULDED BORDERS

Plate XI, figs. 1, 2 and 3
These were drawn from shards found on the site of the Rothwell Pottery in Yorkshire. A few plates with these borders have been found.

Plate XI, figs. 4, 5 and 6
Shards of plates with these borders were found on the site of the Melbourne Pottery in Derbyshire (Plate 47A). Shards of fig. 5 were also found on the site of the 'W.B.' (perhaps William Bacchus) factory at Little Fenton, Staffordshire.

Plate XI, figs. 7, 8, 9, 10, 11 and 12
These are examples of 'feather' borders found on plates and dishes of various factories. Fig. 7 is that used by Josiah Wedgwood. Fig. 8 is the Melbourne variety, of which a great many shards were found on the pottery site. Small Melbourne plates have a border closely resembling fig. 7. Fig. 9 is the Rothwell version, shards of which were found on the Rothwell Pottery site. Shards of fig. 10 were excavated at Little Fenton on the site of the 'W.B.' factory (see p. 84). Figs. 11 and 12 are specimens of Leeds feather borders. Although most factories consistently used one pattern of feather border the Leeds Pottery seems to have used several. There were, of course, many other varieties of this border used by other factories. Fig. 12 will be seen to be in reverse. It was the usual practice on sauceboats for the border to run from the handle to spout necessitating a reverse pattern on one side. On two-handled sauceboats the pattern ran from the handles towards the centre on both sides. This pattern does not seem to have been produced at the Cockpit Hill factory.

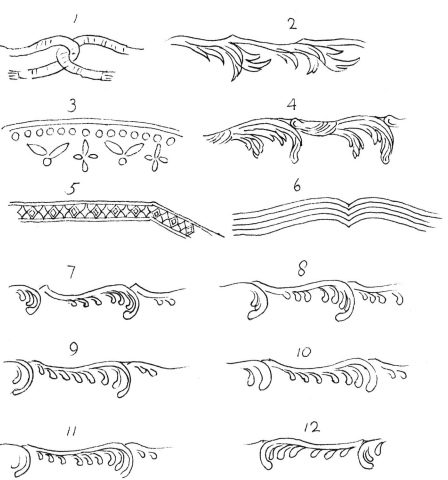

XI Creamware Moulded Borders. *See page 212*

Appendix II

PATTERN AND DRAWING BOOKS

THE LEEDS POTTERY PATTERN AND DRAWING BOOKS

The Leeds Pottery issued its first pattern book in the year 1783. This was reprinted in 1794. A second edition with more plates was issued about 1800 and this was reprinted in 1814.[1] The title page of the first pattern book bears the following inscription:

> Designs of Sundry Articles of Queen's or Cream Colour'd Earthenware manufactured by Hartley, Greens & Co., at Leeds Pottery with a great variety of other Articles. The same Enamell'd, Printed or Ornamented with gold to any pattern; also with Coats of Arms, Cyphers, Landscapes, etc. etc. Leeds 1783.

The pattern books contain plates with engraved illustrations. A list describing the plates was issued under separate cover. The 1783 edition contains forty plates, the articles being numbered from 1 to 152 followed by 1 to 32 for tea-ware. The second edition contains thirty-one more plates, the new designs being numbered from 153 to 212, and 33 to 48 for tea-ware.

There are three Leeds drawing books at the Victoria and Albert Museum entitled 'Original Drawing Book No. 1', 'Original Drawing Book No. 2', 'New Teapot Book'. These consist of drawings and designs pasted into old account books of the Leeds Pottery. Some of the accounts are still visible, but are for the most part difficult to decipher. The following entries, however, occur frequently: 'Ordered at Swinton, to be marked etc.', 'Ordered from Swinton to come here'. These show the close connection between these two Yorkshire potteries and indicate that at least some of the marked pieces were destined for the Swinton Pottery. These drawing books date from about 1778 to 1792. The date 1778 occurs on the drawing of a mug with a scroll handle. The 'New Teapot Book' though undated seems to date from about 1790 to about 1820. The designs which are in colour include the following patterns:

[1] The second edition of the Leeds pattern book is reproduced in its entirety in *The Leeds Pottery*, by Donald Towner, London, 1963. For further details of the Leeds pattern book see *Leeds Arts Calendar*, No. 56, 1965.

Green-glazed vertical bands.

Reeded horizontal bands filled in with green glaze.

Underglaze-blue pagoda patterns.

Enamelled sprays of flowers in red, black and green.

Enamelled 'Chinaman in a garden' pattern.

Cloudy and mottled glazes.

Granite wares.

Cream-colour banded with deep orange-buff.

Bright blue ground with small chequered borders of black and white.

Many formal patterns in mineral colours of brown, buff, sage-green and a
soft deep blue.

A large number of border patterns resembling those painted for Wedgwood
at his Chelsea workshops.

Landscapes, and a series copied from Thomas Bewick's wood-engravings.

The following drawing books are in the Leeds City Museum and Art
Gallery:

Drawing Book No. 1, dated 1781. Although this book is labelled No. 1 it is
unlikely that it is the first as the drawings contained in it are numbered from
153 to 272. Some are coloured.

Drawing Book No. 2, dated 1803. The drawings numbered from 274 to
375.

Drawing Book No. 3, dated 1814. Drawings numbered 401 to 457.

Drawing Book No. 4. No doubt the last, as it is undated and the drawings
unnumbered. It contains seventy-five drawings.

Handle Drawing Book, about 1805. Nos. 1–27.

Black Ware (Basalt) Drawing Book, dated 1800. Nos. 1–90.

Enamel Table Service Drawing Book (in colour), about 1800–20.
Nos. 1–301.

Enamel Tea Ware (in colour), 1819. Nos. 1–90.

Ornamental Drawing Book No. 1, dated 1801. Nos. 1–29.

The first four of these books contain many of the original drawings from
which the engravings were made for the pattern books, as references beside the
drawings show. A copy of the Leeds pattern book, now in the Leeds City Art
Library, gives prices for the various articles depicted and has forty-six pen and
wash drawings and eleven water-colour drawings in addition (see *Leeds Arts
Calendar*, No. 67, 1970).

THE WEDGWOOD CREAMWARE PATTERN BOOKS

Wedgwood's 'First Pattern Book', which is now at the Wedgwood Museum,
Barlaston, was begun about 1770. This book contained drawings for use within
the factory and was not published. Additions to the book were made

continuously until the year 1814. Included among the designs are patterns in colour for the borders of the early Queen's ware.

In 1774, Wedgwood first published a creamware pattern book. This was entitled 'A Catalogue of the different Articles of *Queen's Ware*, which may be had either plain, gilt, or embellished with Enamel Paintings, manufactured by Josiah Wedgwood, Potter to her Majesty'. This pattern book consisted of nine engraved plates which depicted thirty-five different articles of creamware. A descriptive list of these articles was issued on a separate sheet and both the list and the book of engravings were sent out together in boxes which also contained actual specimens of creamware.[1] This pattern book is of great rarity but is reproduced in Harry Barnard, *Chats on Wedgwood* (London, 1924) and in Jean Gorely, *Old Wedgwood* (Wellesley, Mass., 1942).

If the designs contained in the Wedgwood and Leeds pattern books be compared the differences of design between the wares of the two factories will, in most cases, be strikingly apparent.

In 1774, Thomas Bentley prepared a catalogue of the famous creamware service made for the Empress Catherine II of Russia, which consisted of nearly a thousand pieces. The title of the catalogue reads: 'Catalogue and General Description of a Complete Service of Porcelain or Queen's China Ornamented with Various Views of Ruins in Great Britain, Country Seats of the Nobility, Gardens, Landscapes and other Embellishments, All painted in Enamel & Executed According to the Orders and Instructions of the Most Illustrious Patroness of Arts the Empress of all the Russians, By Her Imperial Majesty's Very Humble and Most Grateful Servants Wedgwood and Bentley, London, 1774.'

Two further books of Queen's Ware, known as 'Shape Books', were produced in 1803 and in 1817 for use within the factory. The illustrations for the 1817 shape book were engraved by John Taylor Wedgwood and William Blake the artist and poet, and consist of patterns for table, kitchen and dairy ware. This book also contains designs in colour for border patterns.

In addition to the creamware catalogues, Wedgwood published a number of catalogues of ornamental stoneware.

THE CASTLEFORD POTTERY PATTERN BOOK

A copy of this book in the Victoria and Albert Museum is written in both French and Spanish. It contains fifty-seven plates and 259 engraved designs. Many of these show considerable differences of design from the Leeds patterns. The title page has the following inscription: 'Desseins des pièces de Fayence fabriquées à Castleford Pottery près de Leeds par D^d. Dunderdale & Co. 1796.' From this pattern book it is apparent that although the double

---

[1] A version of this pattern book and list, written in French, and containing thirteen plates of engraved designs, is at the Wedgwood Museum, Barlaston.

intertwined handle was a usual feature of the creamware of the Castleford Pottery, it generally ended in a foliate shape and neither the applied terminals, which were such a feature of the handles made by the Leeds Pottery, nor the flower knob, seem to have been made at Castleford to any extent. The usual form of knob made by this factory seems to have been one shaped like an onion. Knobs shaped as fruit were also used.

THE WHITEHEAD PATTERN BOOK

James and Charles Whitehead of Hanley published a pattern book in 1798 with the following heading: 'James and Charles Whitehead *manufacturers* Hanley Staffordshire.'

The title page reads:

> Designs of Sundry Articles of Earthenware. At the same Manufactory may be had A Great Variety of Other Articles, Both useful and ornamental as well Printed, Painted & Enamelled as likewise Dry Bodies such as Egyptian, Black, Jasper etc., etc. Birmingham, printed by Thomas Pearson 1798.

The Explanation of the Plates was printed in English, Dutch, French and German. There are very few distinctive patterns in the book. They seem to be derived very largely from other pattern books, such as Wedgwood, who seems to have been their biggest customer, Leeds and Castleford. Few pieces have been identified so far, but a cruet and a pair of candlesticks are here illustrated (Plate 34A and B).

Pattern books were also produced by the Swinton and Ferrybridge potteries.

Appendix III

MARKS

Enoch Booth of Tunstall, Staffordshire (see page 23)

1. Incised and filled in with cobalt blue on the front of a scratch-blue saltglaze mug at the Fitzwilliam Museum, Cambridge (see Bernard Rackham, *Early Staffordshire Pottery*, London, 1951, Plate 54).

2. Incised and filled in with cobalt blue on the front of a scratch-blue loving-cup, at the Hanley Museum (see J. C. Wedgwood, *Staffordshire Potters*, London, 1914, Plate facing page 68).

3. Painted in underglaze blue, beneath a creamware bowl at the British Museum (Plate 1A and B).

Cockpit Hill, Derby (see pages 90–104; see also marks 188, 189 and 193)

4 and 5. Transfer-printed in black by Thomas Radford on a creamware teapot at the British Museum (Plate 38A). These and other variations, for

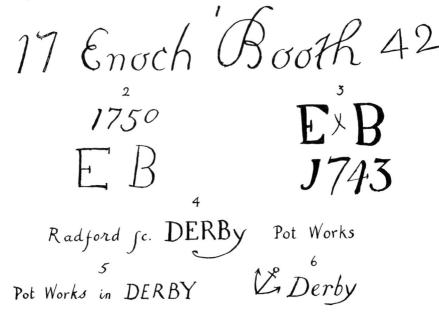

example 'T. Radford Sc. Derby', are the marks of the engraver Thomas Radford and are sometimes found on transfer-printed specimens of Cockpit Hill creamware.

6. Transfer-printed in black on Cockpit Hill creamware (Plate 38B). The anchor mark is usually ascribed to Richard Holdship (rebus for 'hold ship').

Leeds Pottery (see pages 119–159; see also mark 181)

7. Impressed. Length 1⅛ inches.[1] This is probably the first mark to be used by the Leeds Pottery, and occurs on a shell sweetmeat-dish of a deep cream-colour, made before 1775, in the author's collection (Plate 57A). The different style of lettering from the later marks should be noted.

8 to 11. Impressed. These are the usual marks which occur on Leeds creamware made after 1775 and approximately before 1790. These marks vary in length from 1⅛ to 1¼ inches. The asterisk, full stop and hyphen are used in varying positions, but their significance is not known. The set-up of the letters is not mechanically exact; the mark is often slightly curved. Numerals impressed in larger type may refer to sizes.

12. Impressed. Length 1¼ inches. This mark which is in a different type was used by the Leeds Pottery about 1790.

13. Impressed. Length 1⅛ inches. This mark usually occurs on Leeds Pottery figures made between approximately 1780 and 1800. The type is slightly irregular and it is sometimes impressed twice on a single piece.

14. Impressed. Length 1 inch or less. This mark, in which the type is compressed, is believed to have been used by another factory working at Leeds during the nineteenth century and is not the mark of the original factory. Creamware with this mark is often decorated in underglaze-blue painting. It also occurs on some figures of horses.

15. Impressed. Length 1 inch. The type is straight and regular. This mark was used at the Leeds Pottery on creamware from approximately 1800 till 1820. It also occurs on creamware of more recent date. Some pieces with this mark have the year 1915 impressed on them, and were sold during the 1914–18 war in aid of Queen Alexandra's Red Cross Fund. Such pieces differ considerably from the original creamware of the old pottery. Over-elaboration of pierced decoration is usual; the glaze is more glassy and differs in colour from the original glazes; the crazing on such pieces is of a different character to that on the original creamware and sometimes covers the entire piece; the modelling is less sharp and the general appearance often looks dirty and lacks the brilliance and the life of the original ware.

16, 18, 19, 20 and 21. Impressed. These marks were used by the Leeds Pottery on creamware made after about 1800.

17. Transfer-printed. This mark occurs on some of the engravings made at

[1] Measurements are taken in each case between the left-hand serif of the 'L' and the right-hand serif of the 'Y' or to the punctuation mark beyond the 'Y' if such exists, but does not include any numeral following.

the Leeds Pottery for transfer-printing upon creamware (Plate 79A). Some transfer-printed pieces having this mark are also impressed with one of the impressed marks 8 to 11 or mark 22.

22. Impressed or enamelled. This mark impressed is a factory mark of the Leeds Pottery dating from approximately 1780 till 1820. The letters 'LP' enamelled in blue occur on one corner of the saddlecloth of a figure of a horse, about 16 inches high, at the Yorkshire Museum.

23. Impressed. This mark is occasionally found on creamware made at the Leeds Pottery towards the end of the eighteenth century. Though it may stand for 'Green', it is more probably a workman's mark.

24. Transfer-printed in blue or other colours (quoted by Kidson). This was probably the last mark to be used by the Leeds Pottery and was the mark of Richard Britton and Son, 1872–8.

25. Incised. This mark occurs on a candelabrum at the Victoria and Albert Museum. This piece consists of an urn-shaped vase with winged female figures on either side. Metal branched candle-holders were originally inserted between the wings. It is illustrated in the original pattern book of the Leeds Pottery, No. 116, and in J. and F. Kidson, *Historical Notices of the Leeds Old Pottery* (Leeds, 1892, Plate 15). Some very close copies of this piece were made on the Continent. As the mark consists of the letters 'LP' combined in a monogram, it may be a factory mark, but no other example is at present known.

26. Impressed. This mark is sometimes found stamped underneath the covers of teapots, coffee-pots, tea-caddies, covered jugs, etc. These pieces show the finest quality of potting, material and workmanship and are decorated with flowers painted in crimson enamel or gilt. The terminals to the double intertwined handles and flower knob are touched with green. There is little doubt that pieces with this mark are all from one service and were made by the Leeds Pottery. This service has been erroneously ascribed to the factory at Temple Back, Bristol, but a mark of that factory was 'MH', not 'HM'.

27. Impressed, occurs on some pieces of Leeds creamware. An impressed 'spade' mark also occurs on some creamware made at the Swansea factory.

28. Impressed. This mark was sometimes impressed on Leeds creamware of an early date. It also occurs on moulds from the original Leeds Pottery, which are now at Temple Newsam House, Leeds.

29. Impressed. A large centre-piece of a slightly grey colour, at the Leeds City Art Gallery is impressed with this mark. The probable date of this piece is about 1860. Kidson quotes this mark as being used at the Leeds Pottery during the period of Richard Britton's ownership (1853–78).

30. Incised, on some deep cream-coloured ware believed to have been made at Leeds before 1775.

31. Incised. This mark occurs in conjunction with the impressed mark 'LEEDS * POTTERY' on pieces of creamware, green-glazed ware and tortoiseshell ware. It is very doubtful whether such pieces are the products of the original Leeds Pottery.

7
LEEDS•POTTERY

8
LEEDS•POTTERY.

9
LEEDS•POTTERY 2ſ

10
LEEDS POTTERY●

11
LEEDS POTTERY–

12
LEEDS•POTTERY.

13
LEEDS POTTERY,

14
LEEDS–POTTERY

15
LEEDS.POTTERY

16
HARTLEY GREENS & Co.
LEEDS * POTTERY

17
Leeds Pottery.

18
HARTLEY GREENS & Cº
LEEDS * POTTERY

19
LEEDS•POTTERY.
LEEDS•POTTERY.

20
HARTLEY•GREENS&Cº
LEEDS•POTTERY

21
HARTLEY GREENS&Cº
LEEDS•POTTERY
HARTLEY GREENS&Cº
LEEDS•POTTERY

22
LP

23
G

24
R.B. & S.

25
ℒ

26
HM

27
♤

28
☽

29
ℒ

30
4

31
\\/

32
Wood
O
1803

33
B J ſ

34
Samuel
Bawd
1769

35
GREEN, LEEDS,
1768

36
✕

37
LEEDS POTTERY

32. Incised, in conjunction with the Leeds Pottery mark No. 8, impressed twice on a pearlware puzzle-jug at the Leeds City Art Gallery (see Donald Towner, *Handbook of Leeds Pottery*, Leeds, 1951, No. 90). The name 'Wood' incised in similar handwriting also occurs on some pearlware oval-shaped teapots enamelled in colours, which were made about 1800.

33. Incised; these marks occur on a mould for sauceboats from the original Leeds Pottery and now at Temple Newsam House, Leeds. The impressed

crescent combined with a large incised letter 'B' and other marks which are undecipherable occur on a teapot illustrated on Plate 22B in *English Cream-coloured Earthenware*, by Donald Towner.

34. Incised on a deep cream-coloured screw-top box at the Fitzwilliam Muséum, Cambridge, probably manufactured in the Leeds district.

35. Incised, on a creamware plaque fitted into the base of a Wedgwood creamware coffee-pot, at the Leeds City Art Gallery. No such mark was used by the Leeds Pottery.

36. Incised. This mark occurs in conjunction with the Leeds Pottery impressed mark No. 8, but is also found on Wedgwood creamware.

37. Impressed. Length $\frac{7}{8}$ inch. The mark 'LEEDS POTTERY' without any punctuation marks, mostly occurs on cream-coloured ware of recent manufacture some of which is semi-translucent.

38

Greatbatch

39

Published as the Act directs Jan? 4 1778
by W. Greatbatch Lane-Delf Staffordshire.

39a

William Greatbatch, Engraver, Lane Delph, Staffordshire (see pages 34–42)

38 and 39 (Plate 36B). Transfer-printed in black. These marks sometimes occur on creamware teapots which are transfer-printed in black and coloured over in enamels (see page 40).

39A. Impressed mark of William Greatbatch (see page 40).

Josiah Wedgwood (see page 72; see also marks 183 to 187)

40 to 46. Impressed. There were many slight variations of type and spacing in the Wedgwood marks on creamware made before about 1775, which are exemplified by the marks 40 to 46. Some of these will be seen to be in lower-case letters beginning with a small 'w', others are in lower-case letters beginning with a large 'w'. Some are in capital letters, but all are irregularly spaced. These marks were often used in conjunction with workmen's marks. The pieces illustrated in this book on which the marks 40 to 46 occur are shown on the following plates:

40. combined with 61, Plate 18B.
41. combined with 78, Plate 26A.
42. combined with 63 and 75, Plate 24.
43. combined with 60, Plate 16A.
44. Plate 22A.
45. combined with 64, Plate 25.
46. combined with 56, Plate 13A.

47 and 48. Impressed. These are the first regular marks. 47 has the 'O's widely spaced and oval in shape, 48 is in lower-case letters. They seem to have been used on creamware made between approximately 1770 and 1775.

49. Impressed. This was the mark extensively used by the Wedgwood factory from about 1775.

50. Impressed. This mark is sometimes found impressed on the back of figures made to Wedgwood's order by the Wood family at Burslem (see page 72). The mark from which the illustration was taken occurs on a large creamware bust at the Victoria and Albert Museum by Enoch Wood. The word 'SADNESS' is impressed on the front. The mark No. 50 varies in size according to the size of the figure upon which it is impressed. The irregularities of the letters themselves also vary slightly.

51. Impressed. The Wedgwood mark used in conjunction with three letters (of which mark 51 is an example) was introduced in 1860. The first letter indicates the month, the second letter indicates the potter's initial or mark, and the third letter the year in which the piece was made. The sequence of letters standing for the year began with the letter 'O' for 1860 and continued in sequence through the alphabet to 'Z' for 1871 and then began with 'A' for 1872 and continued through the entire alphabet to 'Z' for 1897. The year 1898 was indicated by 'A', and the cycle was repeated, 'Z' standing for 1923.[1]

52. Impressed. The letters of this mark will be seen to be more widely spaced than the normal mark. It was impressed on whiteware made about 1840. Such ware is usually very light in weight.

53. Impressed on some pieces of pearlware from about 1780.

54. Impressed. The word 'ENGLAND' was added to the normal mark in 1891.

55 and 56. Enamelled. These marks frequently occur under pieces of deep cream-coloured dessert-services. Such pieces are usually painted with flowers in purple or crimson (Plate 14A) and are sometimes impressed with mark No. 46, as well. Marks 55 and 56 were enamellers' marks, the letter 'B' standing for Bakewell (see page 58).

57. Printed in colour. This mark was introduced in 1940, and is used on the present-day creamware made by Josiah Wedgwood and Sons, Barlaston.

---

[1] A complete list of date marks, which includes the month as well as the year, is set out in J. P. Cushion, *English China Collecting for Amateurs*, London, 1967, and J. P. Cushion, *Pocket Book of British Ceramic Marks*, 1976.

58 and 59. Impressed potters' marks. These two marks are of frequent occurrence on Wedgwood creamware made during the eighteenth century.

60 and 61. Impressed potters' marks. These marks are sometimes found in conjunction with the early impressed factory marks and were in use before 1775. The teapot on Plate 16A is impressed with marks 60 and 43, that on Plate 18B, with marks 61 and 40.

62 and 63. Impressed potters' marks. 62 combined with 48 and 67 is impressed on a cake-basket at the Victoria and Albert Museum; 63 combined with 42 and 75 is impressed on the covered jug shown on Plate 24.

64. Impressed potter's mark. This mark used in conjunction with 45 is impressed under the coffee-pot shown on Plate 25.

65. Impressed potter's mark. This little mark is of frequent occurrence on Wedgwood's eighteenth-century creamware. It is sometimes found impressed, as on the coffee-pot shown on Plate 19.

66. Impressed potter's mark, which is sometimes combined with the normal impressed factory mark.

67. Turned. A circular mark formed by a tool in the centre of the base of a piece of creamware while it was being turned, is of frequent occurrence on the wares of the Wedgwood, Leeds and other factories.

68. Incised. These letters which almost certainly stand for Josiah Wedgwood, occur on the base of a cauliflower-ware tea-caddy in the Victoria and Albert Museum. The caddy is not creamware in the strict sense of the word but of a common earthenware. It is possible that the initials are those of John Wedgwood, John Warburton, or Jacob Warburton, but the style of letters exactly corresponds with Josiah Wedgwood's handwriting.

69 to 74. Impressed potters' marks which sometimes occur in conjunction with the normal Wedgwood impressed factory mark on eighteenth-century creamware.

75 and 76. Incised. These are two of the earliest potters' marks to be found on Wedgwood's creamware. 75 occurs in conjunction with 42 on the covered jug illustrated on Plate 24. These marks would appear to date from about 1765.

77, 79, 80 and 81. Impressed, eighteenth-century potters' marks on Wedgwood's creamware.

78, 83 and 84. Incised, eighteenth-century potters' marks on Wedgwood's creamware.

82. Incised. This mark occurs on the eighteenth-century creamware of both the Wedgwood and Leeds factories.

In addition to marks 40 to 82, which occur on Wedgwood's creamware, a circular stamp containing the words 'WEDGWOOD AND BENTLEY ETRURIA' is sometimes found on the stoneware base of creamware vases made in imitation of stones (Plate 27). This mark never occurs on creamware itself.

Other Yorkshire Potteries (see pages 160–9)

85 and 86. Impressed on creamware and green-glazed ware, are marks of

40
Wedgwood

41
Wedgwood

42
wedgwood

43
Wedgwood

44
WEDGWOOD

45
WEDGWOOD

46
WEDGWOOD

47
WEDGWOOD

48
Wedgwood

49
WEDGWOOD

50
WEDGWOOD.

51
WEDGWOOD
ADR

52
WEDGWOOD
ETRURIA

53
Pearl

54
WEDGWOOD
ENGLAND

55
B

56
g

57
OF ETRURIA
WEDGWOOD
MADE IN
ENGLAND
& BARLASTON

58
V

59
B

60
○

61
C

62
♡

63
⬡

64
✳

65
O

66
⬯

67
○

68

69
□

70
◇

71
∷

72
[

73

74
||||

75
W

76

77
a

78
||

79
ω

80
◇

81
C

82
X

83
√

84
h

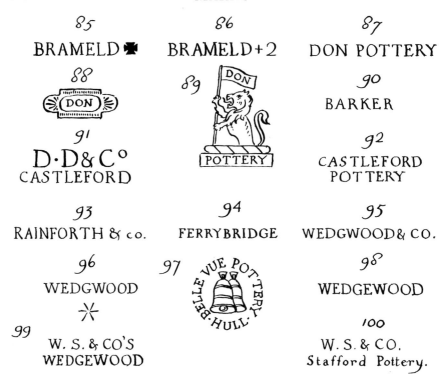

85
BRAMELD ✱

86
BRAMELD + 2

87
DON POTTERY

88

89

90
BARKER

91
D·D & C°
CASTLEFORD

92
CASTLEFORD
POTTERY

93
RAINFORTH & co.

94
FERRYBRIDGE

95
WEDGWOOD & CO.

96
WEDGWOOD

97

98
WEDGEWOOD

99
W. S. & CO'S
WEDGEWOOD

100
W. S. & CO.
Stafford Pottery.

the Swinton Pottery (see page 160). L. Jewitt in *Ceramic Art of Great Britain* (London, 1883), quotes mark 85 followed by an additional cross. The impressed mark 'BRAMELD' in capital letters without any additions also occurs.

87 to 90. Impressed, are the marks of the Don Pottery at Swinton (see page 162).

91 and 92. Impressed, are the marks of the Castleford Pottery (see page 162).

93. Impressed. This mark was used from 1800 at the Hunslet Hall Pottery, Leeds (see page 166).

94 and 95. Impressed, are the marks of the Ferrybridge (Knottingley) Pottery (see page 166).

96, 98, 99 and 100. Impressed, are the marks of the Stafford Pottery, Stockton-on-Tees (see page 168).

97. Impressed, is the mark of the Belle Vue Pottery at Hull. Sometimes the lettering is omitted from this mark (see page 168).

John Daniel of Cobridge and Burslem (see page 32)
101. Incised. This mark occurs on a creamware cake-basket and stand at the British Museum. It is decorated with pierced open-work and is of a rich cream-colour.

101

John Daniel 1775.

102

Neale & Co

103

NEALE & Co

104

Neale & Wilson

105

WILSON

106

NEALE & BAILEY

107

C

108

CC

109

C

Neale and Co. of Hanley (see pages 73–4)

102 (Plate 29A) and 103. Impressed marks used by this factory before 1786.

104, 105 and 106. Impressed marks used by this factory after 1786.

107, 108 and 109. Impressed. These marks were used by Wilson who was John Neale's partner from 1786. They are sometimes erroneously stated to have been used by the Leeds Pottery.

The Wood Family of Burslem (see pages 78–80)

110, 111 and 112. Impressed. These are the factory marks of Ralph Wood of Burslem, senior and junior. 112, which is stamped in low relief, is a rebus for 'wood'. This and 110 are sometimes to be found on the earlier figures and may therefore be the marks of Ralph Wood senior (Colour Plate C); whereas 111 occurs on the later figures and may be considered the mark of Ralph Wood junior (Plate 31).

113. Impressed. This is almost certainly a mark of Enoch Wood (Plate 32).

114 and 115. Impressed, are also marks of Enoch Wood, and were probably used between 1783 and 1790.

116. Impressed. The partnership mark of Enoch Wood and James Caldwell, which was used between 1790 and 1819.

Elijah Mayer of Hanley (see page 76)

117 and 118. Impressed marks.

William Adams of Greengates, Tunstall (see page 80)

119 and 120. Impressed marks.

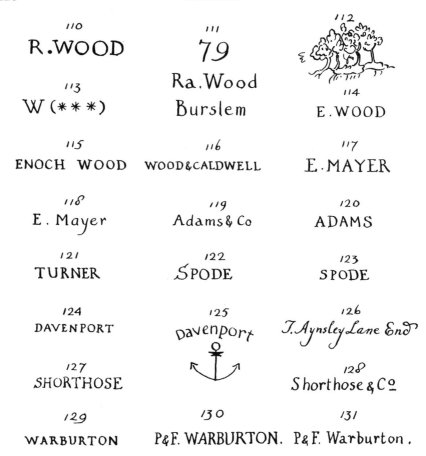

110
R.WOOD

111
79
Ra.Wood
Burslem

113
W (* * *)

114
E.WOOD

115
ENOCH WOOD

116
WOOD&CALDWELL

117
E.MAYER

118
E. Mayer

119
Adams & Co

120
ADAMS

121
TURNER

122
SPODE

123
SPODE

124
DAVENPORT

125
Davenport

126
J. Aynsley Lane End

127
SHORTHOSE

128
Shorthose & Co

129
WARBURTON

130
P&F. WARBURTON.

131
P&F. Warburton.

John Turner of Lane End (see pages 74–6)
121. Impressed mark (Plate 30A).

Josiah Spode of Stoke (see page 82)
122 and 123. Impressed marks.

John Davenport of Longport (see page 82)
124 and 125. Impressed marks (Plate 33).

John Aynsley of Lane End (see page 76)
126. Transfer-printed. John Aynsley was an engraver. It should not be assumed that he manufactured the ware on which this mark occurs.

Shorthose and Heath of Hanley (see page 80)
127 and 128. Impressed marks, sometimes combined with an impressed crescent.

132 Sadler Liverpool

133 Green, Liverpool

134 Abbey, Liverpool

135 R. Abbey, sculp

136 Rd. Abbey, Sculp

137 Johnson

138 Jn. Johnson Liverpool

139 Billinge sculptor Liverpool

140 HERCULANEUM

141 SEWELLS & DONKIN D

142 SEWELL & DONKIN

143 SEWELL

144 ST. ANTHONY'S

145 FELL

146 T. FELL & Co.

147 FELL NEWCASTLE

148 PHILLIPS & CO.

149 DIXON & Co. Sunderland Pottery

150 DIXON AUSTIN & Co.

151 MOORE & Cº Southwick.

152 SWANSEA

153 DILLWYN & COM. 10

154 DILLWYN & Co

158 Bristol Pottery

155 S

157 Ω

156 C

159 J. Eaves   Bristol

160 Absolon Yarm

161 Y

162 Absolon yarm N25

Peter and Francis Warburton of Cobridge (see page 89)

129, 130 and 131. Impressed. Marks 130 and 131 occur on creamware figures, and some cruets which have a central figure (Plate 31). Such pieces are of the finest quality. Mark 129 occurs on whiteware vases in the neoclassical style, which may have been made by another branch of the family, and on some plain creamware.

Liverpool and Other Creamware Factories (see pages 170–80)

132 and 133 (Plate 22B). Transfer-printed. These are marks of Sadler and Green, a firm of printers at Liverpool who were responsible for most of the printing on Wedgwood's creamware (see page 172).

134 (Plate 90A), 135 and 136. Transfer-printed. These are the marks of Richard Abbey who engraved for Sadler and Green in the first place but started business on his own account in 1773. These marks probably date from this time (see page 170). Mark 136 occurs in conjunction with mark 138 on a teapot at the Castle Museum, Norwich, probably made by Joseph Johnson of Liverpool.

137 and 138.   Transfer-printed. Joseph Johnson of Liverpool appears to have been both an engraver and a potter (see under mark 136); the mark, in most cases, probably relates to the engraving only (see page 172).

139. Transfer-printed. The mark of Thomas Billinge, an engraver of portraits at Liverpool (see page 172).

140. Impressed. A mark of the Herculaneum factory at Toxteth Park, Liverpool (see page 174; see also mark 191).

141, 142, 143 and 144. Impressed, are the factory marks of Sewell and Donkin of the St. Anthony's Pottery, Newcastle-upon-Tyne (Plate 92A) (see page 174).

145, 146 and 147. Impressed, are the factory marks of Thomas Fell of the St. Peter's Pottery, Newcastle-upon-Tyne (Plate 92B) (see page 174).

148, 149 and 150. Impressed, are the marks of Dixon, Austin, Phillips and Co. who worked a pottery at Sunderland. They produced a coarse whiteware decorated with lustre, transfer-prints, etc., which cannot be considered creamware except in the very widest sense (see page 176).

151. Transfer-printed, on some of the ware made at the Southwick Pottery on the River Wear (see page 176). This pottery was founded in 1788 by Anthony Scott, who produced a coarse whiteware with transfer-printed and lustre decoration, which cannot be considered creamware, except in the very widest sense.

152, 153 and 154. Impressed. Factory marks of the Swansea factory (see page 180).

155 and 156. Impressed. Factory marks of the Swansea factory (see page 180). Mark 155 was sometimes painted in red enamel.

157. Impressed. A potter's mark of the Swansea factory (see page 180).

158. Transfer-printed. This mark occurs on some transfer-printed ware made at Joseph's Ring's factory at Temple Back, Bristol, about 1802 (see page 178) (Plate 93B).

159. Enamelled. The mark of an enameller at Joseph Ring's factory, Bristol (see page 176).

160, 161, 162. Enamelled. These marks occur on creamware made by Davenport, Turner and other factories. They were the marks of Absolon, an independent enameller at Yarmouth (see page 76) (Plate 33).

Continental Creamware (see pages 181-7)

163 and 164. Impressed. Charles and Jacob Leigh, Douai, France.

165. Enamelled in red. Chantilly, France.

163
LEIGH

164
DOUAI

165
ꞆOᴬ

166
CREIL

167
MONTEREAU

168
LA CHARITÉ

169
A DW

170
DURLACH

171
WEDGWOOD

172
H

173
HOLITSCH

174
MB
Sten

175
F.D.V.N.

176
G.M
B

177
K

178
• • •

179
Jacques Boselly

180
BG

166 and 167. Impressed. Clark and Shaw, Creil and Montereau, France (Plate 96B).

168. Impressed. Peter and Francis Warburton, La Charité-sur-Loire, France.

169. Impressed. Joseph Wouters, Andenne, Belgium.

170. Impressed. Durlach, Germany.

171. Impressed. Hubertusberg, Germany.

172 and 173. Impressed. Holitsch, Hungary.

174. Impressed. Marieberg, Sweden.

175. Impressed. Vecchio family, Naples, Italy.

176. Impressed. Giovanni Maria Baccin, Le Nove, Venetia, Italy (Plate 95).

177. Impressed. Johann Ehrenreich, Königsberg, East Prussia.

178. Painted in brown. Gudumlund, Denmark.

179. Painted in red. Giacomo Boselli, or Jacques Boselly, enameller, Savona, Italy.

180. Impressed. Biagio Giustiniani.

Additional Marks

181. Leeds Pottery impressed mark.

182. Impressed on shards excavated at Little Fenton (Fenton Vivian), believed to be the mark of William Bacchus of Fenton Vivian (see page 84).

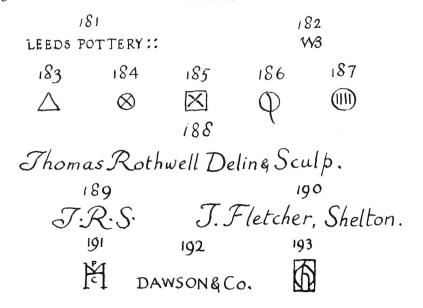

181
LEEDS POTTERY ::

182
WB

183   184   185   186   187

188

Thomas Rothwell Delin & Sculp.

189   190

J·R·S·   J. Fletcher, Shelton.

191   192   193

DAWSON & Co.

183, 185, 186 and 187. Impressed marks on early Wedgwood creamware.

184. Painted in black under some early Wedgwood teapots.

188 and 189. Transfer-printed on a Cockpit Hill teapot at the Fitzwilliam Museum, Cambridge.

190. This signature is found transfer-printed on the wares of various factories, and refers to the engraver only.

191. An early impressed mark of the Herculaneum factory (see page 174). 'H' and 'M' stand for the first and last letters of Herculaneum; 'P' and 'C' for Pottery Company. It occurs on plates etc. often transfer-printed in overglaze black with a lady and two children walking in a garden.

192. Impressed or transfer-printed. The mark of the Ford Pottery, South Hylton, Sunderland, founded in 1800 by John Dawson (see page 176) (Plate 93A).

193. Impressed in imitation of a Chinese seal mark sometimes found under Cockpit Hill teapots with a pineapple in relief on the sides (Plate 46A).

BIBLIOGRAPHY

Simeon Shaw, *History of the Staffordshire Potteries*, Hanley, 1829

Eliza Meteyard, *The Life of Josiah Wedgwood*, London, 1865

Llewellyn Jewitt, *Ceramic Art of Great Britain*, London, 1878

Joseph and Frank Kidson, *Historical Notices of the Leeds Old Pottery*, Leeds, 1892

Maud Sellers, *Pottery, A History of the County of York* (Victoria County Histories, Vol. II), 1912

J. C. Wedgwood, *Staffordshire Pottery and its History*, London, 1914

Oxley Grabham, *Yorkshire Potteries, Pots and Potters*, York, 1916

W. J. Pountney, *The Old Bristol Potteries*, London and Bristol, 1920

Arthur Hurst, *Catalogue of the Boynton Collection of Yorkshire Pottery*, York, 1922

Emil Hannover, *Pottery and Porcelain* (translated from the Danish by Bernard Rackham), London, 1925

Bernard Rackham, *Catalogue of the Schreiber Collection*, Vol. II, London, 1929

F. Williamson, *The Derby Pot-Manufactory known as Cockpit Hill*, Derby, 1931

Bernard Rackham, *Catalogue of the Glaisher Collection* (Fitzwilliam Museum, Cambridge), Cambridge, 1934

W. B. Honey, *Wedgwood Ware*, London, 1948

E. Stanley Price, *John Sadler, a Liverpool Pottery Printer*, West Kirby, 1948

Bernard Rackham, *Early Staffordshire Pottery*, London, 1951

Donald C. Towner, *Handbook of Leeds Pottery*, Leeds, 1951

W. B. Honey, *European Ceramic Art*, London, 1952

Wolf Mankowitz, *Wedgwood*, London, 1953

Geoffrey Godden, 'Derby Pot Works, Cockpit Hill' in *Transactions of the English Ceramic Circle*, Vol. 3, Part 4, 1955

Donald C. Towner, 'The Leeds Pottery, Jack Lane, Hunslet', in *Transactions of the English Ceramic Circle*, Vol. 3, Part 4, 1955

Donald C. Towner, 'Some Creamware Comparisons', in *Transactions of the English Ceramic Circle*, Vol. IV, Part 3, 1957

Donald C. Towner, *English Cream-coloured Earthenware*, London, 1957

Donald C. Towner, *The Leeds Pottery*, London, 1963

Donald C. Towner, 'David Rhodes Enameller', in *Transactions of the English Ceramic Circle*, Vol. 4, Part 4, 1963

Donald C. Towner, 'William Greatbatch and the Early Wedgwood Wares', in *Transactions of the English Ceramic Circle*, Vol. 5, Part 5, 1964

Donald C. Towner, 'Leeds Pottery Records', in *Transactions of the English Ceramic Circle*, Vol. 6, Part 3, 1967

Alan Smith, *Liverpool Herculaneum Pottery*, London, 1970

Donald C. Towner, 'The Cockpit Hill Pottery, Derby', in *Transactions of the English Ceramic Circle*, Vol. 8, Part 1, 1971

Donald C. Towner, 'The Melbourne Pottery', in *Transactions of the English Ceramic Circle*, Vol. 8, Part 1, 1971

Donald C. Towner, 'Some Leeds Enamellers', in *Transactions of the English Ceramic Circle*, Vol. 9, Part 2, 1974

Heather Lawrence, *Yorkshire Pots and Potteries*, Newton Abbot, 1974

Peter Walton, *Creamware and other English Pottery at Temple Newsam House*, Leeds, 1976

INDEX